Confessions of a Scholarship Judge:

How to Win More Scholarships by Understanding what the Judges HATE

by Josh Barsch

CEO, GiveMeScholarships.com

Chapter I

The Most Basic and Fundamental Rule

Please, please, please: Just follow the instructions. Many of the tips you'll read about in this book are very specific, but this one I'd consider more as a very general "rule to live by" – at least as far as scholarship applications go. It's a cliché that rules are made to be broken, but don't be tempted; the rules that a committee places on a scholarship are not there to be broken. They're there for you to follow, and for good reason.

Did you ever wonder why, for example, most scholarship essay contests put a word limit on the essays you have to write? Is it simply a test that rewards the most succinct of writers? Not really. It's something much simpler than that. Essays have word limits to make the task of reading all of those essays manageable for the busy committee members.

Now, you may read the title of this section and snicker at its minimal title to simply "Follow Directions." Duh. Of course we know to follow directions, you say. We're not stupid. Who would actually waste their time going to the trouble of filling out a scholarship application just to ignore the instructions?

A good question, and four years ago, I would've been as incredulous as you. But not now. The answer to that question is: Thousands and thousands of students do exactly that, every single month. They either screw up or thumb their nose at the instructions in dozens of ways. And by now, even though I'm used to it, it doesn't cease to amaze me. Want some examples? Good, because I've got plenty:

Example A: The length of your essay. We'll start with this one because it's commonly abused. While I've never met a scholarship judge who actually sat down and counted every word to ensure that an applicant didn't go over the limit, you still must stick to that limit. If an essay calls for 750 words or less and you send in five single-spaced pages, you either didn't read or simply didn't care about the instructions. When you do that, you're sending us one or more of the following messages, none of which makes us happy.

What you're saying: I feel my essay is perfect, and any alteration of it would soil its perfect form. It simply cannot be edited further.

What the judges say: Even the world's most accomplished writers -- Pulitzer Prize winners, best-selling authors, etc. -- have editors. One task these editors must perform is to cut out words, paragraphs and pages that aren't necessary. It's hard sometimes, but it has to be done. If you can't do it, get a friend, parent, teacher, English major, or someone else to do it. But it can and must be done, because otherwise, your application gets thrown in the trash. And we don't mean it gets thrown in the trash like your 3rd grade teacher would threaten to do if you forgot to write your name on your paper -- we really, honestly throw it in the trash. Actually it's the shredder, since it's got your personal information on it. But you get the message.

What you're saying: Yes, my essay is too long, but that's too bad, because I have some REALLY important things you need to hear.

What the judges say: Most of the people who apply for this scholarship have some really important things to say, and they say those really important things within the allotted word limit. That's what you have to do, too, if you want a chance to win. Think of the rules like a basketball game: regardless of how badly you want to win, you can only have five people on the court at one time. You can't throw two or three extra people out there, because then you'd have an advantage that no one else has. That's cheating and it's not allowed.

What you're saying: I didn't realize I submitted an essay that was too long; I didn't read the instructions.

What the judges say: If you're not going to read the instructions, then we're not going to read your essay. Sorry.

Example B: Sending your essay the wrong way, in the wrong format, to the wrong place, to the wrong person, etc. Back in the days when we required our scholarship applicants to send in paper applications (we now do it all via email), we posted a very clear statement in the instructions: "Please do not send your essay via signature-required delivery." By signature-required delivery, we simply mean when places like FedEx, UPS, DHL and the U.S Mail make you sign for a delivery. If this sounds unimportant, believe me, it's not.

Remember that many scholarship programs get thousands and thousands of applicants. We understand that you'd like to make sure your essay arrived safe and sound, but there's a reason we prohibit this: If even a few students per day require signature delivery on their application, then that's several daily interruptions for the unlucky soul who's getting the applications. Imagine if every day, DHL rang your doorbell at 9 a.m. and made you sign for three envelopes, and then at 1 p.m., UPS rang your doorbell and made you sign for three more, and then at 2:30, FedEx came by and made you sign for five more. And then, worst of all (big surprise here) is the U.S. Post Office. If a signature delivery is sent to a PO Box (which is often the type of place we like to have you send your scholarships, to separate them from other business at our workplace), then you actually have to *take a number and stand in line* to retrieve the mail. If you live in a rural area, this is not a big deal; however, if you live in anything even close to a large city, you know that these lines can easily spell a 30-45 minute wait. Sometimes longer.

So, to recap: sending signature-required mail equals a DHL visit, a UPS visit, a FedEx visit and a possibly maddening visit to our local post office. Every...single...day, until the application period is over. Remember Rule #2, Judges Are Busy People. Sending signature-required mail when you're specifically asked not to is a sure way to get your application discarded. As for our company, we simply stopped signing for the packages, and therefore they were either sent back or discarded by the delivery company.

Example C: Sending information you weren't asked to send. This one is less clear to the layperson, so I'm going to lay down the law for you right here and now, so there's no confusion. If you aren't asked or invited to include additional information with your application such as transcripts, photos, newspaper clippings, artwork, CDs, letters of recommendation, trinkets you've whittled out of driftwood or anything else, don't include it.

Why not, you ask? Wouldn't it be something extra to help swing the judges' opinion in your favor? Perhaps so, and if the instructions invite you to do so (for example, by telling you that you may include "any other information you feel is relevant" to the award), then do so. But if the instructions say, basically, "fill out the application and return," then that's not an invitation to stuff the envelope with photocopies of every accomplishment and award you've won since the third-grade spelling bee. Everything we mentioned above, we've received, and then some (OK, not the driftwood – that was a joke). I'm not saying you shouldn't be proud of things like this (because you should), but they don't belong in scholarship applications where they aren't required.

Example: We once got a CD from a student who apparently was quite accomplished at playing the piano, and he'd played all the songs on the CD. I'm sure they were nice songs, but I can't tell you for sure, because we didn't listen to it. And to be honest, even if we had listened to it, I wouldn't have known whether the guy was a good piano player; I'm not in a position to judge. I can't even play "Chopsticks." Point is, our scholarship was an essay contest, and because of that, we feel obligated to judge our students by their essays, period.

The first problem with "envelope-stuffing," as I'll call it, is Rule #2: Judges are busy. When they sign on to judge a scholarship competition, they're expecting to evaluate the applicants based on the criteria of the contest. If it's an essay contest, we expect to be reading essays, and that's it.

The second problem is that submitting additional items is unfair to the other students who actually followed the rules. How fair would it be that the rule-breaker gets to submit an envelope full of additional support for the committee to consider, but the students who follow directions to the letter are only judged on the application itself? This book and the all the supporting materials that came with it are all about giving you an "unfair advantage," but it's a fine line; if you take too many liberties, you'll alienate the judges and get tossed.

BOTTOM LINE: Whether it's the length, topic, or format of the essay or anything else, observe the instructions faithfully.

Part II

The Visual Appearance of Your Essay

Use a standard font size. Although the appearance of each font will differ, usually a standard size is 11 or 12 point (by way of comparison, this book is written in 12-point Trebuchet MS, and it's written for easy reading, not essay-style formatting). If you go any bigger than 12, your essay starts looking like a billboard. The only reason I can surmise that anyone would be using a font size bigger than 12 is that they are attempting to make a short essay look longer than it is (perhaps trying to meet the requirement of, say, a five-page essay when you've only got three and a half pages). If this is the case, please trust me on this: you're fooling no one. If you've reached the point in your life where you're acting as a scholarship judge, that means you've probably written hundreds, if not thousands, of essays in your life – essays with those same page limits, requirements, etc.

We've been there before, monkeying with the font size ("Bump it up to 14 and see how that looks!"), the line spacing ("You think they'll notice if I use 2.5 spacing instead of just double spacing?"), the leading, the kerning, putting a header and footer on each page, pushing the horizontal margins in, pushing the vertical margins down, etc. You name it, we've probably done it. Not only that, but when your essay comes up for review after dozens of others who *didn't* fool around with formatting tricks, then yours will stand out like the proverbial aching digit.

On the other hand, if you go smaller than 10, things get difficult to read. Remember that, in most cases, these same committee members who know all the spacing tricks are quite a bit older than you, and for a lot of them, their eyesight isn't what it used to be. Ever watch your grandpa struggle to read the TV Guide? (Do people still buy the TV Guide? I'm not sure. If they do, they're sure to be grandparents.) And if they can't read your essay, they can never find out how great and worthy of scholarship money you actually are. That's why it's important to keep the font at a reasonable size.

If possible, use a laser printer instead of an inkjet printer. Ink smudges easily; toner doesn't. It's that simple. And the more committee members there are putting their grubby little fingers all over it, the more likely an inkjet-printed essay is to get smudged up and ugly. If you print your essay with a laser printer, it's got a better shot of staying in pristine condition until the judging is done.

Laser printers aren't nearly as hard to come by as they used to be. In fact, prices are coming down so low that inkjet printers will probably be extinct in five years. In the last six months, I've seen laser printers priced as low as $79. If you can swing that, pick one up for your home use, and you can use it for everything you write.

Footer function of Microsoft Word or similar programs. You just open a header or footer (no need to do both), and insert your name and click a button to automatically insert the page number on each page (it varies depending on which program you're using).

Chapter III

The Packaging of Your Essay

You must Beat the Stack. Once you read this section, it'll seem very obvious, but most people completely overlook the advantage you can give yourself by paying great attention to the way you physically package your essay. Remember Rule #1: Competitors are everywhere, and you must put your best foot forward. Your essay's packaging is one way to do this that hasn't even crossed the mind of most of your competition; hence, it's an area where you can seize a big advantage if you give it your best effort.

First, though, let me give you a little bit of background on the nuts and bolts of what happens to your scholarship essays once you send them in. Where do you think they go? You've probably never given it much thought, and rightly so. You're much more concerned with winning the contest and collecting the cash. I can't blame you.

In most cases, the scholarship essays go in a) a big pile; b) a big file cabinet; or c) a big pile inside a big file cabinet. If you imagine the committee eagerly rips them open and reads them the moment they come in -- sorry, it doesn't happen that way. Most scholarship judges have day jobs, and during the day, that's what they do -- their day jobs. Usually, we just set aside big blocks of time later on down the line, closer to the end of the application period (often after the application period has passed) for reviewing applications. And like other normal people, we often procrastinate as the stack grows bigger and bigger.

Consequently, you as the scholarship applicant face one of the most difficult challenges around: you must beat The Stack. That's what we're going to call this phenomenon from now on in this book: Beating the Stack. You've got to find some way, any way at all, to somehow make your piece(s) of paper stand out from the thousands of others in that stack. If Confessions were a human being, his purpose in life would be to help you Beat the Stack.

Submit your essay in a large envelope. Preferably a 9"x12" or even a 10"x13"envelope so that you don't have to fold or otherwise crumple your essay to get it to fit. After all, you'll be going to a lot of trouble to make sure your essay has a very nice appearance, and you don't want to let it all go to waste by folding it up into a small envelope and letting it sit with the post office for a week.

Don't use clear plastic page protectors, and for that matter, the long triangular binders that come with them. First of all, these are a pain to read -- it makes turning the pages difficult, and as far as that goes, trust me, staples are just fine! More importantly, though, a plastic cover for every page of your essay prohibits us scholarship judges from doing one thing that we very much like to do, and that's write on your essay! Maybe it's an asterisk marking your essay for more consideration later (in other words, a possible winner instead of one bound for the trash), or maybe it's a note to another judge to "Read this one first, it's very well done" or some other thing. In any case, we can't do it if the pages are in plastic protectors. That's overkill. Don't do it!

Send your essay in a folder so the papers stay crisp. Remember when I said that using high-grade paper was one of the best dollar-for-dollar ways of making your essay stand out? Well, this tip is in the same category as that one, but this one may be even better.

Let's examine what happens to your essay after you drop it in the mail (or even if you send via UPS, FedEx, etc.). Surely you've already heeded my earlier advice about putting your application in a large envelope that prevents you from having to fold it. But even then, it still has quite an ordeal to endure before it gets into our hands.

It's going on a brutal trip across the country that begins when it's picked up and tossed into a document bin on a truck. Then, it gets taken back to an office, where it's dumped somewhere else into another box and eventually loaded onto a plane or semi truck (depending on how you sent it). With the higher-end delivery services, it's then going to a sorting facility where it's going to be tossed around with millions of other packages on conveyor belts and tons of other sorting machinery. Then it reaches its destination city, where it's tossed onto a truck again, and then, if you're lucky, maybe the delivery guy won't fold the thing in half and shove it in our mail slot.

Keeping pieces of paper in good shape from point A to point B isn't easy, is it?

But you have a weapon at your disposal -- a high-quality folder. They're sold at Office Max, Office Depot, Staples, even Wal-Mart and the like. Get a good-quality, glossy folder (I like glossy ones myself, just because they look even sharper than the cheap-o folders, and they might run you a whopping 50 cents more) and put your essay/application inside it.

Even one of the flimsy, 6-for-a-dollar folders will keep a few sheets of paper safe from creases, tears, and rips, but you've come this far already, so don't go cheap-o on me now. Go the whole nine yards and buy a thick, glossy folder. Trust me.

Here's a secret for you: Essays that arrive in folders tend to stay in their folders as they're passed around from judge to judge. Don't ask me why; it's just one of those tendencies about human beings that seems to be innate. I do it myself. Something inside me says that when I pull a nice essay out of a nice glossy folder, then I ought to put it back in that folder when I'm done with it. So not only will it stay protected from the delivery folks, it's very likely to stay pristine as it gets handed around between judges.

And like I said earlier about the high-quality paper, an essay in a folder stands out from the thousands of others that aren't. That's probably the single best thing about this trick: almost no one does it. That's why you should -- it gives you a great little edge and is a great tactic for Beating the Stack.

Chapter IV

The Content of Your Essay

your friends, there are lots of other kids you don't know who are doing the same thing. No one knows better than us -- we've got stacks of applications lying around from kids who are saying the same thing.

The moral of the story, then? Don't talk about others, just talk about you. The judges will already be comparing you to all the other kids -- you don't need to remind us.

Don't be afraid to admit your past shortcomings and explain how you turned things around. Sometimes, the best story you have to tell a committee will involve explaining some of your worst or most embarrassing moments. Maybe you hurt or insulted someone close to you. Maybe you had an addiction or even went to jail. If you're still hurting your loved ones, addicted or making frequent trips to jail, then you may want to choose a different topic.

But if you've become a better person and conquered these kinds of obstacles, then that's the sort of human progress that scholarship committees like to recognize and encourage further with monetary awards. And admitting your shortcomings also shows humility, which is another favorite trait among winners, in our experience. So if you've got to dip into your dark side to show how your bright side emerged, don't be afraid to do so.

(Note: This depends, really, on how dark your dark side really is. If your dark past includes any serious violent or sexual crimes, then it's probably best to talk about something else.)

Balance pride with humility. This can be tough, since just about every scholarship essay you'll ever write is asking you to trumpet all the qualities that make you deserving of free money. But think about it – you've known lots of people who were very, very good at certain things. Some you hated, and some you admired – probably because of how they balanced pride with humility. We can find some easy examples in the world of sports.

While Dallas Cowboys wide receiver Terrell Owens has a lot of fans in Dallas, he's easily the most reviled player in the NFL by players and fans alike. Is it because he's great, and everyone is just jealous of his greatness? No – he's definitely great, but so was Jerry Rice, who was beloved and respected by nearly everyone. The difference is this: Owens does everything he can to embarrass his opponents while he's dominating them. But Rice, who understands his own greatness just as well as Owens understands his, respects his opponents and does not "rub it in." It isn't that Rice doesn't know how good he is, and it isn't that he's not proud -- he just balances that pride with humility.

Using another example, when did you last see Mia Hamm taunt a goalie after scoring? Never. She's the most prolific scorer in the history of women's soccer and never once has let her pride trump the fact that she was just happy to be there. In your essay, you've got a much better chance at winning if you temper your pride in your achievements with some humility. Bragging turns off more people than it impresses.

Avoid references to perfection. Some of the most tired, overused phrases we see in essays is that of "striving for perfection," "perfecting my skills," etc. Leave perfection alone – you're never going to achieve it. No one ever does. And even if they did, no one would recognize it. This may seem like nitpicking, but there's already too much emphasis on perfection today. Do the best you can, and be proud of the level at which you arrive. Musing about your pursuit of or brushes with "perfection," however, has been known to arouse a snicker in more than a few judges over time. Remember, "nobody's perfect," and it's going to stay that way for a long time.

But of course, you're still striving; after all, the law of the jungle says that the moment you stop moving is the moment you get eaten, right? Fair enough, and you definitely ought to be talking about this in your application. Just adjust your language to indicate that you're trying to be all you can be, to fulfill your potential, to use your talents to the fullest, etc. -- rather than trying to be "perfect."

Stay on topic. In other words, exclude any unnecessary information that has nothing to do with your essay. Everything in your essay should be relevant to the topic at hand. We receive bad examples of staying on topic every day. They're the essays that start like this: "My name is Jane Doe, and I was born in Hershey, Pennsylvania on July 3, 1986. My mother is a dental hygienist and my father is a mortgage broker, and I have two brothers and two sisters. I attend Kennedy High School, where I am a senior."

Unless you're somehow going to tie that information into some critically important part of your essay, the committee doesn't care a lick about any of it; instead, it sounds suspiciously like you're trying to fill up space on the page and nothing more.

Unless you're bringing up things like your birthplace, parents and siblings in order to shed light on your unique upbringing – as in the old "Tobacco Road" song that goes, "I was born in a trunk, momma died and my daddy got drunk and left me here to die alone" – then info like this is a waste of space and a waste of the committee's time. We call it "commodity information." Everyone has a birth date, a school and a hometown, and unless yours have some sort of special significance, leave them out of your essay.

Don't talk solely about your participation in common high school activities. This is an important tip that you'll rarely hear, but it's true. Remember what was said at the outset of this book: The Internet has opened scholarship opportunities up to thousands of applicants who wouldn't have been there 10 years ago. And that means the less unique your essay is, the more likely it is that you'll be passed over for the scholarship. So four years of science club, soccer team, dance team, school play and varsity band is going to end up as a blur to the committee. They see literally hundreds of essays come in with that same stuff in them every single day. Not even a scroll of AP classes and high SAT scores are going to set you significantly apart from your competitors.

So, are you a slacker for doing the things that high-achievers around the world do? Of course not. I'm just telling you straight out that listing your participation in the clubs and sports and activities found in most high schools across the country is probably not going to be good enough to make you stand out. You'll have to dig for something deeper, better, more unique.

How, you say? Keep reading.

Show some industry. Talk about what you've actually done – not just the groups you've joined. Sure, you were in your church's youth group. And you can put "Four years in my church youth group" in your application if you want. But if you do that, you're not telling me much. Since I haven't been to your church, I don't know what your church's youth group does. For all I know, you could be building full-scale models of Noah's Ark and doing research at the Dead Sea, or you could all be taking a one-hour nap every Sunday. I have no idea. You have to tell me.

Set yourself apart, then, by talking about what you did over that time. Let's say you spend four years in your church youth group serving meals to the homeless one day a week in a soup kitchen. Maybe you served an average of 150 people on each of those days in the soup kitchen (it's OK to give an honest estimate -- you're not expected to be exact on matters like this). There are 208 weeks in four years, and that means you served 31,200 meals to homeless people during high school.

Now *that's* impressive. But I'd have never known about it if all you put on your scholarship application was "Spent 4 years in church youth group," now would   I? If you want us to know you're industrious, you have to tell us what you've done. That makes the difference between a boring, commodity essay and one that makes the committee's eyes pop.

Don't be preachy. Scholarship essays are certainly about self-expression, and lots of applications ask open-ended questions about how you, the forward-thinking leader of tomorrow, might solve today's problems. That gives you full license to come out with your ideas on how to change things, and in so doing, you'll probably find yourself pointing out the flaws of society -- i.e., the things that need to be changed. But be careful about getting on a "high horse" and sounding too judgmental or preachy, or giving the impression that solutions to the world's problems are *obvious*.

Let me point out why this is important. There are legions of intelligent young people out there, but maturity eludes many of them. Intelligence is cheap. Maturity is priceless. If I had to choose a single most important quality in scholarship winners, it would be maturity. Show maturity in your essays and you'll be much more likely to bring home a check.

Why is this? It's because you're headed into a make-or-break stage of your life when you hit college. The things you do there -- even seemingly small things -- will have an immense, life-altering effect on your life. And it's maturity, not raw intelligence, that is your key to handling those situations successfully. You may be a wizard at literature or science or economics or whatever, but if you can't handle the pressures of the world, you're likely to flame out and not meet the goals you have for yourself right now.

As scholarship judges, we don't want to give money to people who are going to flame out. We want to give money to the ones who are going to make it. Hence, we look for and place great value on maturity. Got it? OK.

So, how do we tell who's mature and who's not? Well, it's an inexact science, to be sure. But one of the hallmarks of maturity in young people is their ability to balance their own big ideas with the knowledge that the world is complex, and that they still have a lot to learn. The world is a complex place, and solutions to society's most difficult problems are hard to find. That doesn't mean you can't help solve them someday; it just means that, if we're talking about a real problem, it's not going to be easy to solve.

With that in mind, if you catch yourself writing overly simplistic phrases such as, "If more people would just..." or "The world would be a better place if we would just wake up and realize," remember that the problems you're talking about probably don't have solutions as simple as you think. I'm not positive, but few major problems have ever been solved by a collective bunch of folks all spontaneously "waking up and realizing" anything. Your scholarship judges are educated and know this all too well. Preachy proposals will likely lead to some eye-rolling when your essay is being read, and that's not good for you.

Go easy on the slang, yo. Every generation uses a great deal of slang, but it's usually not the same slang the previous generation used. And it's most likely that the committee evaluating your essay isn't from your generation. One recent applicant mused about his football career and "leaping for a pick and taking it straight to the house." If you watch SportsCenter on ESPN, you know that our applicant meant he intercepted a pass and returned it for a touchdown. But guess how many of our committee members watch SportsCenter religiously? Not many.

Be careful with sensitive political issues. We almost didn't include this tip, but it's one that every applicant needs to hear. Unless the scholarship you're applying for is sponsored by an explicitly liberal or conservative organization, you have almost no chance of winning if you write in a partisan way about controversial issues like abortion, affirmative action, the Iraq war or any other polarizing issues. Why not, you ask? Surely it takes guts and conviction to write such an essay, no?

Yes, it does. And let me be the first to say that I've got a ton of admiration for people, students and otherwise, who stick to their convictions and lay their neck out on the line with an unpopular opinion, regardless of who it might offend.

However, I didn't write this book to tell you how to speak your mind. I wrote it to show you how to win money from a group of people who will sit in judgment of you and thousands of your peers (hey, we're called judges for a reason). And I submit to you that essays about contentious issues usually don't win.

More practically, consider this very basic truth: the more contentious the issue you choose to write about, the more likely it is that one or more committee members will completely disagree with you. Divisive issues divide, and in all likelihood, you've got no idea who's even judging your scholarship application, let alone the personal and political beliefs of those people. But if a judge happens to hold beliefs that run counter to the ones in your essay, should that affect their judgment?

In a perfect world, absolutely not. But we don't live in a perfect world, and if you happen to find one, email me and I'll meet you there for margaritas for the rest of eternity. Remember Rule #2: Committee members are people just like you and me. They try to keep their emotions and personal beliefs out of their decisions, but it doesn't always work.

Offend them with the content of your essay and you probably won't win the scholarship. Again – I'm not saying it's right, but that's just how it is. It's real life, it's unfair, and that's how it goes. Rather than pretending otherwise, I'm advising you to acknowledge this reality and go the safe route with safe topics when you have a choice.

Writing about hot-button, partisan issues is like serving veal as the main course at a banquet. Some people will love it, but others will scream and yell until you wish you'd just chosen the bland old chicken dish that everyone's just lukewarm about. When it's all said and done, you've got a better chance of winning the scholarship writing about chicken than about veal.

Be careful talking about religion. See above. Same reason, times 10. I'm not going to repeat everything I said above, but one thing I will: I didn't write this book to tell you how to say what's on your mind; I wrote it to tell you how to win. It's fine to have religious convictions and no one can ever take them away from you, but it's also one of the quickest possible ways to offend the sensibilities of that one judge who doesn't agree with or looks down on your religion. Once again – it may not be right, but it's true. You don't have to disavow any religious convictions you might have, and it's not that you can't make any reference to them at all -- it's just a safer route not to make them the crux of your entire essay.

Don't dwell on your GPA - it's not a point of distinction. Nothing angers the high-ranking students (and their teachers) more than this one, but Uncle Josh has some bad news for you, and you're not going to like it. However, you do need to accept it because it's true, and I know it's true because I write the scholarship checks and your teachers don't. Are you ready? Are you sitting down? OK, here goes:

Your GPA doesn't really matter that much. If at all.

It's ok, I'll give you a minute to let it sink in.

Now, here's why this is true:

A nationwide grade-inflation epidemic has killed the significance of a high GPA. Thousands of pages have been written on this topic over the last 10 years, and I won't rehash them all here. But I'll summarize:

At some point in the recent past, someone decided that the horror of seeing the letter "D" or "F" on a report card did much more long-term damage to a kid than, say, not knowing how to read, write or spell. Lots of parents agreed, and convinced schools that even though Johnny still doesn't know what a comma is, he still deserves a B in English..

Anyhow, the point is this: Nowadays, just about everyone has a GPA of 3.0 or above. Everyone. So what, you say? Well, that means if everyone has a similar GPA, then **nobody's GPA matters anymore.** That's it, plain and simple – if everyone's GPA is the same (or close), what's the point of even looking?

Yes, but: I can hear it already: "Yes, but today's students are smarter than ever! Classes are more advanced, students are better prepared, and their achievements get more outstanding every day. It makes sense that the GPAs are higher."

It's absolutely true about the students being smarter than ever, and the achievements, and all that. The stuff that today's top students know and master and achieve is just mind-boggling. Considering the latest generation has been pushed harder than ever – and earlier than ever – by parents to achieve great things, makes it no surprise. But that just proves the point: if the best students are even better today than before, then why does everyone look the same on paper? If it weren't for the grade inflation phenomenon, the top students would stick out more; but as it is, they simply don't.

And last but not least, the quality of education in our country varies so widely that a 4.0 student (or, in some cases, a 5.0 or higher) at one school might flunk out at another. It also works the other way; a solid B-C student at a rigorous academic high school may have the brains to blow through the system with a 4.0 or better at a weaker school.

Thousands of students apply for our scholarships annually, and almost every one has a GPA of at least 3.0 on a 4.0 scale. That's fine; it's certainly better than having a GPA of 1.0 or 2.0. But one phenomenon remains the same: when nearly every applicant shares a particular characteristic, then that characteristic becomes unimportant – and that's the story with GPA. Are we saying not to include your GPA? Not necessarily, especially since many scholarships require you to report it. But don't dwell on it in your essay, or expect it to carry you to a scholarship victory. It won't.

Don't forget your family. I know that we miss some incredible stories every day when our applicants write scholarship essays and mention absolutely nothing about the role they play in their own families. Let us say this clearly: your role in your own family is not *as* important as your school activities – it's more important. Hey, let's be honest: School will be over in a few years, but your family is around forever. Members of the cheerleading squad or the football team or the science club will forget your name in 10 years (trust me, it's true -- I've been to class reunions.), but your family never will.

Probably the biggest crying shame in the entire world of scholarships is that, for years, thousands of excellent students have been passed over for scholarships. They are the students who have had no time to participate in extracurricular activities because they had to care for their families or work paying jobs to do so. Worse yet, those students are made to feel like they shouldn't even apply, because they're not "active" enough.

That's the biggest and most unfair load of garbage I've ever heard, and don't let anyone sell it to you. If you're so busy with family responsibilities that you can't involve yourself in student organizations, then you may just have a stronger application than those who do. But remember: We can't give you credit for your family responsibilities if you don't tell us what they are! So by all means, if it's applicable to you, go into detail about how you spend time doing things for your family.

In the particular case of our company's scholarships, we've always given heavy weight to "work ethic," and that's as applicable to those who work hard in their homes and at paying jobs as it is to those who work hard on the varsity field or inside the school walls. Our unwavering advice for scholarship essays is this: Tell your story, regardless of where it takes place.

the committee to cheat on your behalf and possibly commit fraud by essentially turning a real scholarship contest into a pretend scholarship contest with a predetermined outcome. All this, mind you, for a person we didn't even know until they picked up the phone!

Scholarships are a pretty level playing field. They require that everyone follow the same procedure, and may the best applicant win. Calling up and asking for the money outright is the absolute quickest way to ensure that you get none.

Don't act like your life is over if you don't get this one scholarship. Judges know that you would very much like to receive the scholarships that you apply for. It's natural for you to have some emotional stock in whether you win or not. College costs are serious business, and every dime you can get someone else to pick up for you, the better.

But in thousands of applications over the years, we've seen applicants taking this to extreme levels. Time after time, students write that if they don't receive this very scholarship, they probably won't be able to attend college. Or they won't be able to pay the rent, or they'll be kicked out into the streets (I'm not exaggerating here).

Now I admit that one of my purposes in writing this book is to help you manipulate the scholarship judges and, where appropriate, play on their emotions to your advantage. But remember, it's a fine line. You must be careful about how hard to try to tug on the judges' heartstrings. There are a couple of reasons why laying on the desperation in a scholarship essay is a bad idea:

1) It puts undue and unwelcome pressure on the scholarship committee. Judges are human, and no one wants to feel like the person who flushed a kid's educational dreams down the toilet, or

worse yet, got you tossed out of your apartment and onto the streets. Committee members have a heart, but they also have a job to do, and that's to select the most qualified applicant. By suggesting that you won't make it without them, you put them in a bind. How? Well, you're not the only one doing it! There are a dozen stories a week just like these. And when there's one scholarship to give and 12 people (this week) who say they can't make ends meet without the award, then it's a lot easier for the committee to trash all 12 and get back to its job of selecting the most qualified applicant.

2) From a more practical standpoint, you should never depend on receiving any one scholarship. The odds are always stacked against you (although less so, now that you're a Confessions owner), and placing your hopes on one award is like putting all your money on one roulette number. Always have a backup plan. Always investigate all your student loan options, grants, jobs, etc. Even someone with all the inside info in this book shouldn't bank on receiving scholarships if at all possible. Develop your educational plan first, including costs and how to pay for them; then, as you receive scholarships, start erasing sources of funds like loans and jobs as they're no longer needed.

Don't act like you're owed the scholarship. It's rare, but still regular, that we get applicants who will explicitly state that they are very obviously the best candidate and that the committee will most certainly agree when they've finished reading his/her materials. Well, maybe. And maybe not. Don't get us wrong, confidence in life is generally a good thing, but there's a fine line between confidence and arrogance. And remember, the committee likes humility better than swagger. I'm not sure why that is, but it just is.

There's a Part 2 here as well, and that's the person who insists the scholarship is owed to them not necessarily because of their achievements, but because they're currently going through a rough patch in life. These applicants say that because they've recently lost a job, come up short on money for their first-choice college, moved into an expensive apartment, etc., that they *deserve* (their word, not mine) this scholarship.

Well, not really. You deserve a scholarship based on the qualifications the scholarship committee asks for. Sure, we all need an infusion of good luck sometimes, but that doesn't make you deserving of a scholarship. You've got to outshine all the other applicants first!

Complaining about other aspects of your life may resonate with some of the judges, because we too have aspects of our lives that aren't going so rosy at the moment. But there are too many other applicants out there who aren't complaining and ARE putting their best foot forward in their application for anyone to win the competition based solely on the fact that they're having a run of bad luck.

Don't be a complete downer. I debated including this one because, to be honest, a lot of people have had a lot of rotten things happen to them in their lives. More bad than good, unfortunately. And sometimes those things are worth explaining to the scholarship committee if it means you can show them how you've overcome these obstacles on your way to success.

That last part is very important -- the part where you're overcoming these obstacles on the way to success. Very often, though, we get pages and pages of depressing anecdote after depressing anecdote, and then when it gets to the part where the writer is supposed to overcome the obstacles -- the essay ends. Hey, life isn't always rosy – we understand that. But it's a mistake to make your essay a comprehensive study in your personal misery. Here's why:

If you want to win, the committee needs to feel good about handing you money. We want to feel like we're helping someone turn the corner, helping them get out of what was once a bad situation, helping take a person's life from one level to a higher level. But if your essay is one long complaint about your life, the committee doesn't have much reason to believe that one check will change that.

Money is great and we all need it to live, but it's just a means to help you achieve the goals you've set for yourself. If you have no goals, no plan, no outlook for the future, that money will be gone in no time and your life won't have changed a bit.

Don't quote pop-culture icons. We'll talk more about quotes as this book goes on, but here's a good start. If you're going to use a quote, do yourself a favor by not extracting your quote from the pages of *Us* magazine. No Madonna, no Tupac, no Michael J. Fox, no Arnold (even though he's the governor now). It's not that they and their counterparts have never said anything inspirational – they all have. But remember that your audience in the committee is likely much older than you and probably sees Tupac and Madonna in quite a different light than you.

When you quote people from pop culture, it makes you look shallow and poorly educated. It makes you look like you glean your philosophy of life from gossip websites and reality shows, which will not impress your scholarship judges. This may be unfair, of course -- hey, for all I know, Stephen Hawking is inspired by Ludacris and reads Perez Hilton thrice daily -- but that's life, and that's how you're perceived.

Not to mention that the legacy of pop-culture icons can change from day to day. For instance, three years ago you may have used a quote from Mel Gibson that sounded very dignified and profound. However, after his DUI arrest and anti-Semitic tirade, that same quote will be viewed very differently. And once you've put it on paper and sent it in, you can't change it.

You're safer using a quote by a historical figure – the quote will be time-tested and the speaker's legacy secure. Plus, it'll make you look like you actually know some history, which is a lot more rare among scholarship applicants than it used to be.

Don't use overly flowery, exaggerated language. There's a fine line between good, genuine writing and stuff like this: "Receiving this scholarship would certainly be one of the most fulfilling and genuinely rewarding experiences of my life." That's just one example, but there are dozens more we could show you. Here's another: "Receiving this scholarship will be the crown jewel of my accomplishments thus far."

C'mon, enough already with that. We're not THAT gullible. The particular scholarship in question was a $500 scholarship -- an honor and a great thing to win in light of rising college costs, for sure, but not a lifetime accomplishment. Lay off the saccharine language. You know what they say – too much sugar will make you (and the scholarship committee!) sick.

Don't use clichés. Don't write about how you give 110 percent, keep your nose to the grindstone, or how a bird in the hand is worth two in the bush. In terms of creativity, this is about as bad as it gets – these phrases have been used so many times by so many people that they had to invent a special name for them – clichés. You can always do better than a cliché.

Think carefully before using a quotation to start your essay.
Sometime long ago, someone started a speech with, "The Famous So-And-So once said, 'blah blah blah.'" And so began a very, very long love affair with starting speeches and essays with quotes from other people.

I can't completely condemn the practice, because sometimes people do it well. But it's only well-done if the quote you're using *really does* have a great deal to do with what you're writing about. Don't quote "I Have a Dream" if your dream is simply getting enough scholarship money to pay your sorority dues for an entire year. Don't quote FDR's "The only thing we have to fear is fear itself" if the fear you're writing about is the fear that you wouldn't get early acceptance to Boston University. That's not using a quote, it's abusing a quote.

If you quote JFK's "Ask not what your country can do for you, but what you can do for your country" because you've decided to join the military (or an ROTC program, perhaps) knowing of our mounting Middle East presence and the international threats we face in the 21st century, then *that's* a meaningful quote. In that case, you're the very embodiment of the quote you chose, and that's how using quotes ought to be done.

But just ask yourself before you start with a quote: Am I doing this because it applies to me, or just to bolster my essay and sound smarter by quoting someone famous?

If you're going to use a quote, consider a lesser-known, original quote. The most overused quote in the history of the student essay is probably MLK's "I Have a Dream" speech. Second is probably FDR's "fear itself" quote. Using those, or other ones that have been used thousands of times before you, probably won't serve you well. Not only is it unoriginal, but it's a tough act to follow: after quoting the most famous speeches in history, anything you have to say is probably going to sound minor-league at best.

It's easy to find more original, lesser-known quotes on the Internet, as well as the old-school route of actual quotation books. There are many famous quotation websites, many of which have their quotes organized by topic. If you're dead-set on using a quote, use one of these sites to find something original and new. And before you use it, double-check it in different places to ensure that the website you got the quote from is correct about who said it and what was said.

If you're going to use a quote, make it brief. A recent submission from a student in Little Rock included a seven-sentence quote from former President Clinton. That's not a quotation; it's two paragraphs. One or two sentences should be plenty; any more than that is overkill.

Don't draw attention to your negatives; instead, don't refer to them at all. Have I mentioned that scholarship applications are the place to put your Best Foot Forward? Sure I have. They are the pre-college equivalent of a job interview. Usually there's one scholarship available and lots of applicants, just as there's one job opening and lots of applicants. Your job is to convince the people doing the selection/hiring that you are the single best choice for the award/job -- better than anyone else who has applied. Got it? Good.

OK. Now, you may not have been to an interview for a full-time, 40-hours-per-week gig, but your parents probably have. Go ask your dad whether it would be smart to go through an entire job interview that went incredibly well, and then, at the very end as he was getting up to leave, to stick his head back into the interviewer's office to say, "Oh, by the way, forgot to tell you -- I drink alcohol to excess and I can't ever seem to make it anywhere on time. Bye now!" Or, ask your Mom whether in the same situation she'd say, "By the way, I plan to become pregnant in the next few months and then take my full maternity leave, during which I'll tell you I'm coming back, and as my return to work approaches, I'll tell you I'm not coming back at all!"

The answer to those questions, obviously, is no. Those things are your personal business and it would be detrimental to your own plans for you to disclose them to your interviewer. Remember, this process is all about you. You're in it for yourself -- to get the scholarship, to get the job, etc. No need to go shooting yourself in the foot by thinking you've got to disclose every single one of your imperfections. You don't, and you shouldn't.

We've all got weaknesses, and a scholarship essay is not the time to bring them up. The one exception, of course, is if it's a former weakness that you've mastered and want to tell us about. But of all the possible things you could talk about in your essay, your current character flaws probably aren't the smartest choice. If you're failing your math class or you love bar fights or you constantly find yourself kicking puppies, then those are details that you probably want to just leave out, rather than go on about at length and then explain how you plan to fix them.

Avoid laundry lists. Laundry lists are not essays. Essays are coherent papers with a beginning, a middle and an end. If you simply crank out seven paragraphs listing the activities you've been involved in, and for how long you've been involved in them, and the offices you held, etc. -- that's not an essay. It's just a big list in paragraph form. Not only is it not an essay, it doesn't tell the committee very much about you, the person.

Rarely will a scholarship committee reward you for simply listing your activities in paragraph form, regardless of how extensive that list might be. Even if it's an impressive list, there are thousands of students a week who send in lists just as long and impressive. A list alone isn't worth much. You've got to use your essay to breathe life into the list and let the committee know who you are and why you deserve their money!

Omit vanity awards from your list of accomplishments. We're sure to catch heat for this one, but sometimes you have to hear the truth, even if it's an unkind truth. We're referring here to awards such as Who's Who Among American High School Students. The first time you get a letter from Who's Who, it feels great. Someone has told you that you're among the best in the whole country! It happened to us in high school, too. And when we found out that Who's Who wanted $40 for a book with our name in it, we shelled out the $40 and bought that book quicker than you can say "ego boost." If you want to do so, too, go for it. But consider something: How did Who's Who find about you? Did you submit an application to Who's Who? No. But they found you anyway, and without even speaking to you, named you one of the country's most outstanding students. That's a little bit odd, don't you think?

The truth is, Who's Who makes a lot of money by selling books – not by rigorously reviewing the achievements of every single high school student in the nation, comparing them all and deciding who's the best. And the more students they include in their books, the more proud parents and students there are to purchase more books. Students and parents receiving notification from Who's Who for the first time are unlikely to know this; however, those of us who serve on scholarship committees know it all too well.

Therefore, when you put Who's Who (or organizations like them) on a list of your credentials, committee members are going to see that as "padding" – i.e., adding accolades to your application that are supposed to sound good, but really aren't consequential. We recommend omitting Who's Who from scholarship applications/essays.

I feel like I should add something here. No one who's received a letter from Who's Who should now feel like they're not worthy of awards, accolades or recognition. Just because Who's Who sent you a letter doesn't mean you're not worthy of more prestigious awards. And even if Who's Who is the only award you've received, that also doesn't mean that you're not going to achieve every goal you set for yourself in the future. You can, and if you set your mind to it, you will. There are 100 times more successful people in the world than there are award winners.

Don't assume the committee knows your subject of interest as well as you do. You may have deep, intricate knowledge of a particular subject. Maybe it's current environmental issues, maybe it's international news, or maybe it's baseball. You may be tempted to demonstrate your specialized knowledge in a scholarship essay, but be careful. The committee may be old and wise, but they still may not have anywhere near the depth of knowledge that you have on the subject. Don't run too many circles around the committee with an extremely in-depth essay on an obscure subject that may leave them confused.

If you mention a hardship, be sure it's really a hardship. If your parents were killed when you were a baby and you were raised in an orphanage, that's a unique hardship. If you were raised in suburbia and had to share your 2,600 square-foot house with three raucous brothers, that's not. If you had to get a job at age 8 to help your family pay rent, that's a hardship. If you had to get a job at 16 to pay for your first car, that's not.

Making sense yet? Once again, remember that scholarship committees receive thousands of essays from thousands of different backgrounds. Some have had very hard lives and many obstacles to overcome; others have not. If you haven't had to overcome insurmountable odds, that's fine -- that's the case for most of us in the United States, at least -- just don't go to great lengths to make it seem like you have.

Now, a point of clarification: This doesn't mean that just because you weren't orphaned by Sudanese warlords at age 9 that you can't talk about any challenges you've met. You can, and perhaps you should. Judges love to hear about challenges overcome. Just keep your perspective and resist the urge to call these challenges "hardships" or something similarly melodramatic, because trust me -- we've read about every imaginable type of hardship, and we know and appreciate the definition of the word.

If you mention a hardship, say you don't want special treatment (even if you really do). Those who read scholarship essays and choose winners know this: there's a fine line between a story of a person overcoming a hardship and a "sob story." We think one of the differentiating factors is when the writer, either directly or indirectly, suggests that they do not want special treatment or consideration because of their situation. Is this true? Well, probably not – otherwise they wouldn't have mentioned the hardship at all. But practically speaking, the act of explaining a hardship while at the same time stating you want no sympathy is a nice way to protect yourself from the perception of a "sob story."

And remember once again: The key to winning a scholarship on the strength of an essay about hardships is the part where you turn it around and talk about how you've overcome/are overcoming the hardships and are on your way to meeting your goals. Pay attention here -- I'm talking about two different things: overcoming the hardships, and moving on toward other goals. You may have overcome the hardships (congrats!) but may also be sitting there with no goals after having freshly overcome these hardships. That's not gonna cut it. We want a story of overcoming the hardships and movement toward a goal. That's what you need to win the contest with what we refer to as a "hardship essay."

Have you done something unique? Bring it up! If there's one theme of this book, it's that scholarship applications these days are beset with sameness. By and large, there are tons of kids who sound exactly the same writing the same old stuff and claiming the same achievements. That's a little depressing, so let's turn it around: Uniqueness wins scholarships.

Are you an Eagle Scout? Did you climb Mt. McKinley? Are you state champion? A national champion? If you're not, that's OK – most people aren't. But if you are, say so! Even if you're a state champion at making buildings out of popsicle sticks, say so -- don't assume that whatever you're excellent at is too small to mention.

Discuss your social organizations in terms of the service work they do. This is more applicable to college students than high school students, since there's really no high school equivalent of the Greek system of social fraternities and sororities. Simply put, social fraternities and sororities are primarily social organizations, but they also do a lot of charity work. Socializing is fine and dandy -- everyone needs to do it. But it's not particularly impressive on a scholarship application.

Charity work, however, is much more impressive. So if you decide to mention your social fraternity or sorority in your application materials, should you just tell the judges which house you belong to, or should you talk about the specifics of your charity work, and your particular role in that charity work? Which one is going to impress the committee more? Specifics of the charity, of course. Rule of thumb: Be specific. Don't forget it.

As in the rest of the world, opinions vary on the value of Greek life. Most people who were Greeks tend to think highly of it; many of those who remained independent characterize Greeks in a variety of ways, some of them negative. Scholarship judges are no different -- some are hostile to active Greeks, choosing not to look past the booze-soaked parties, hazing and occasional alcohol-poisoning death.

So how do you protect yourself against judges who are inclined to view the Greek system with disdain? Get specific about the undeniable positives of Greek life, namely your charity work. Paint a picture of your Greek life as one of service, and you'll prevent hostile judges' minds from wandering toward togas and date rape.

Committees like it when you've helped people. Maybe it's just human nature, but it does seem like most scholarships end up going to those students who, whether through school, a job, or work outside the classroom, spend time helping other people. Sure, it's still possible to win plenty of scholarships if you don't volunteer, but just take a look at the scholarship winners and biographies that you see posted all over the Web. How many of them specifically mention community service and other feel-good, help-people activities? Quite a few.

If you're already helping others, find a way to talk about it in your essay. If you're not, find a cause that interests you and spend a couple of hours per week doing some work. Not only will it improve the judges' perception of you, it'll also make you feel good.

Committees like stories of overcoming adversity. Scholarship essays are as unique and varied as the people who write them, and the winning essays even more so. But if there's a common theme that judges seem to like (and seem likely to throw money at), it's the theme of someone overcoming adversity in order to succeed in the end.

Doesn't everyone like those stories? That's why we get teary-eyed watching the Olympics – always plenty of feel-good stories there. After all, scholarship judges are regular people like you and me, and who among us doesn't like to feel good?

If you can't think of what to write about, ask yourself – have I ever overcome any adversity? How did I do it? Would others be impressed by it? If the answer is yes, you've got a possible essay topic.

Committees like passion about something, anything. If you're not passionate about your subject, it'll show through in your writing. Passion brings the best writing out of you and those competing with you for the scholarship money. Therefore, if you have the choice, it's best to write about something that you feel strongly about. Your most compelling writing will follow.

There are exceptions to this rule -- religion and other hot-button issues, which I addressed earlier in the book -- but in most cases, passion is a great thing. Passion means you actually *care* about your subject matter. In a society that seems to get more apathetic by the day, true passion is rarer than you might think. Remember what I've said: judges like the rare and unique, and they love passion.

Avoid emphasizing commodity accomplishments. We call things like honor roll and, for college students, the dean's list, "commodity accomplishments." We don't mean to discourage them – we were on them when we were students – but they're commodities. They're a dime a dozen. As mentioned earlier in our previous statements about GPA, nearly everyone who applies for our scholarships is on the honor roll or the dean's list. Does that mean don't mention them? No – it simply means don't spend a lot of time talking about them, because it's unlikely to impress a scholarship committee.

When possible, go into detail. Have I said this before? I believe I have. Most scholarship essays have word limits of some kind, but when possible, don't summarize the most telling parts of your story. Instead, give details. Don't simply say that "I work three jobs to get by." That doesn't tell me what type of work you're doing, how many hours you're working or if it's really that tough of a life you're living.

Instead, say "I work 8-5 at my job as a bank teller, after which I work 7 to midnight as a security guard on Monday, Wednesday and Friday. On the weekends, I work at Blockbuster from 10-6." A description like that leaves no doubt in my mind that you are one busy individual (and also makes me wonder when you find time to go to class!).

Which way of describing your life more accurately depicts how hard you work? And which do you think will earn you more points with the committee?

If you decide to show off your foreign language skills, you'd better come prepared. This is a new tip we created about a few months back after receiving an essay from a young man who was quite confident that he was "completely fluent in Spanish" (those are his words, not mine). He decided to write a couple of introductory sentences in Spanish that were his undoing. Rather than sticking to his native tongue, he tried to explain in Spanish that he was a hard worker. "Yo trabajo muy dificil" is what he wrote – which translates to, "I work very difficult." Not only is he not fluent in Spanish, as he claimed, but he can't even communicate at the rudimentary level. So he was lying to us.

Long story short: if you speak a foreign language, excellent – it's a very impressive skill. If you don't speak a foreign language, then don't pretend you do.

Can't think of what to write about? Ask friends what's impressive about you. If you're the shy type who doesn't know how to blow your own horn, then you're going to find the scholarship application process painful, and especially so when you find out you didn't win any scholarships because you were too timid to tell the world how deserving you are. Scholarships are their own little popularity contest, albeit with a little more merit factored into the equation. Like any time you're asking for money from anyone, the scholarship application requires you to sell yourself to a committee of skeptical onlookers (that would be us, the judges). This ain't the time to be timid or modest. It's time to talk about why you're number one.

If you have difficulty figuring out why you're a good candidate for a scholarship, recruit a friend to tell you why you're worth the investment from the scholarship committee. Sometimes your friends see your best qualities that you miss. After all, that's why they become your friends, right? Because they see the best in you!

Incorporate your minority status if appropriate, but don't make it the crux of your essay. If you're a member of a minority group, you're sure to hear conflicting advice about discussing your minority status in scholarship applications. Some say don't mention it at all; others say get as much mileage out of it as you can. I tend toward the latter, but the problem is, you don't always know when you're going to get mileage by mentioning it.

I don't see any problem mentioning your minority status as long as you don't make it the sole topic of your essay. If you believe you faced and overcame special challenges because of your minority status, then say so and describe those challenges, but don't skimp on the evidence. We get a lot of applications where students mention their minority status and simply *imply* that it was a handicap, that they had to work much harder than others to achieve their goals because of it.

That's certainly true sometimes; other times, maybe not. If your minority status created more work and struggle for you, give us examples. Tell us how. Don't assume, though, that a committee will automatically assign extra merit to your application simply because you are a member of a minority group.

Chapter V
Other Important Yet Hard-to-Categorize Tips

Don't use email smiley faces or any other sort of text-messaging language. "OMG I want this schol soooooooobad! J/K, its all good!"

Now, I'm no curmudgeon. I understand that language, both written and spoken, is constantly changing and that it's young people of every generation who drive a lot of that change. However, most of you realize that the style of communication you use for email, IM and text-messaging shouldn't be the same style you use to communicate with scholarship judges in your application. The language and writing style you use don't have to be stodgy or ultraconservative, but remember – this isn't an email to your best friend, either.

Remember also, from a more practical standpoint, scholarship judges are often quite a bit older than you are, and therefore aren't familiar with shorthand phrases like OMG or J/K and the 300 other ones that younger people use. Even if that style of writing were appropriate for a scholarship essay (and I repeat, it's not!), the judges probably wouldn't understand what the hell you were saying anyway.

If your scholarship application is being sent via email, send it from a neutral or professional-sounding email address. This happens dozens of times a day, so pay close attention here. A committee may love your essay, but you'd be surprised how their impression of you may change once they realize it was sent from demonicsoulslayer420@yahoo.com or gettinmydrinkon@hotmail.com or sexndrugs4ever@gmail.com. If it's not obvious to you that sending email from addresses such as those is not exactly putting your best foot forward, then you should immediately go fill your sink with water and ice cubes, plunge your head into the icy cold and then WAKE UP!

Should it really matter what your email address is if your essay is great? Nope. Does it? Yes. File this one under "life isn't fair." Remember Rule #3 -- the committee pays attention to every little detail. Yahoo!, Hotmail and Google all provide free email addresses - if you don't have a firstname-lastname email address (as in, jennasmith@yahoo.com or roberto.martinez@gmail.com), then go get one from one of those services, and just use it for scholarships and other professional correspondence.

I would even take this a step further. The email addresses I used as examples above all contain some reference to drugs, drinking, sex, etc. -- taboo topics, especially if you're a high school student.

However, I also recommend against sending email from innocent yet still non-professional sounding email addresses: cheerleaderchick@yahoo.com, thebaddest1@yahoo.com, whozyodaddy@gmail.com, gooeylouie@hotmail.com, etc. Basically, any email address that isn't just your name and/or initials, I wouldn't use. It's too easy to just go pick up a free email account and put the issue to rest, and to be sure you're putting your Best Foot Forward.

Don't email your essay as an attachment. We now do a lot of our scholarships via email, and despite our warnings, students still do this occasionally. Here's the problem: if a scholarship program is accepting submissions via email, that means the email address you're supposed to send to is probably sitting on a web page somewhere for you to look at. If it's on a public web page, that means spammers will probably end up taking the address and sending thousands of spam messages to it, and it'll eventually get thousands of viruses sent to it as well. If that's the case, the only safe thing for the scholarship provider to do is simply delete all attachments – all of them. And if you attached your essay as an attachment, because it's impossible to tell what's a virus and what's not. Then your essay is gone.

If you absolutely must send your essay as an attachment (I don't know why that would ever be so, but just in case), email the committee first and let them know your email with essay attached is coming in a separate email that you'll send in five minutes or so. That way, they'll know when it arrives that it isn't a virus.

Have two or more people read your essay before you send it in. They don't have to be smarter than you, or better spellers than you, or anything like that. But you should never send in an essay that hasn't had at least two or three sets of eyes other than your own look over it. They will help you catch errors and other imperfections like the ones we'll talk about below. Here's a point that should shock you: about 85-90 percent of scholarship essays we receive come in with errors of some kind: spelling, usage, grammar or punctuation. Put another way: if you can send in an error-free essay, you rocket yourself into the top 10% right from the start. Hand yours over to a couple of friends and have them help you out.

Language has rules. Abide by them. We don't mean to sound elitist here, but the rules of the English language have already been invented; you can't just make them up as you go along. I could use any of 100 examples here, but one of the most recent examples to cross our desks is this one: "Another importance in my life is my schoolwork." You can't use "importance" like that; the writer should've said "Another important thing" instead. That one should've been eradicated by an English teacher way before this essay got to us. It's OK if you don't know all the rules of grammar and usage yourself, but it's your responsibility to run your essay by someone who does before you send it in.

Learn the difference between "their" and "there," "its" and "it's," "effect" and "affect." Remember how we said that you'd be ahead of 90% of applicants if you just turned in an error-free paper? Well, if you learn these three, you can probably bump it up to 95%. These three distinctions are a) very basic and easy to learn, and b) seemingly screwed up by almost everyone, almost all the time. Lucky for you, I've come through for you with a mini-guide to these phrases, and if you use this guide you'll never screw them up again:

there is the place across from *here*. If you can't point in the direction of "there," then what you really mean is this word...

their, which describes something that belongs to *them.*

It's is a short way of saying *"it is."* If you aren't trying to say "it is," then what you really mean is this word...

its, which refers to anything that belongs to *it.*

And 99% of the time, *affect* is a verb and *effect* is a noun. "Her speeches really *affect* me," but "her words really had an *effect* on me."

Use proper punctuation. Going into detail about all the rules of punctuation would take forever, and frankly, writing a punctuation book would bore me straight into the grave. To be honest, the rules of punctuation are far less well-known that those of spelling and grammar. But if you run your essay by a few people, including an English teacher, you shouldn't have to worry about anything too egregious catching the eye of the committee.

Be grammatical. Just like punctuation, this isn't the place to list all of the rules of grammar. It'd fill a book five times longer than this one. But the more people to whom you show your essay before you send it – and ideally that list includes one English teacher or other grammar wizard – the less likely you'll be to send in an essay with grammatical errors.

Suffice it to say that using good grammar is important, and because so few people use grammar correctly, you'll set your essay apart immediately by doing so.

Use action words. I'm borrowing from my resumed book here, because the advice applies to the scholarship application process just as much as the job-hunting process. When describing the things you've done, use as many strong action verbs as you can. Don't say that you just "went" somewhere, "signed up" for something or "participated" in an event. Say you spearheaded, collaborated, created, organized, mobilized, delegated, supervised, led, etc. Strong action verbs speak loudly! They conjure up images of busy men and women doing a lot of work, and that's what you want the committee to think of when they think about you: a hard worker, buzzing with activity and leading the people around him/her to create. Use those action verbs, and those are the images you'll create in the minds of the judges.

Get to the point! Your introduction should be completed in a paragraph, maybe two. Not four or five. Long-form, scene-setting openings are for novels, not scholarship essays. Get to the point quickly and begin to develop the "meat" of your essay right away.

Don't use redundant language. Redundant language is one particular way of writing badly that wastes your writing space and annoys the committee at the same time. There are a lot of commonly used redundant phrases, but some of the most common are "actively involved" (if you're not active, you're not involved) "past history" (all history is in the past) and "all I can possibly do" (you can't do anything impossibly). Eliminate these phrases from your writing as best you can, because each instance of such phrases chips away at the professionalism of your essay.

Use transitions well. In a nutshell, this simply means making sure your paragraphs flow well from one to the next. There's no magic formula for doing it, but you'll know you've done it when the last sentence of one paragraph seems to lead nicely into the first sentence of the next paragraph. Without good transitions, an essay is choppy and doesn't read well. Do your best to make smooth transitions between each paragraph, and the committee members will be much more likely to enjoy reading your essay.

Make your introduction as creative as possible. So many essay introductions are poorly done (see the next item) that the rare creative introduction stands out a great deal. Challenge yourself to start your essay in a way that grabs the attention of a committee member who has been shuffling through more than 100 essays before looking at yours.

Don't start your essay with "I deserve this award because..." Even if the essay question is "Why do you deserve this award?" it's still a weak introduction. Take your time and introduce yourself and your ideas to the committee in a creative way.

Use a closing. It's disappointing when an applicant is rolling along with an excellent essay, and then all of a sudden, bang! It's over. Or at least, we think it's over. We don't see a next page, so we assume it must be over. The reason for our confusion is the writer's lack of a closing. A closing is the natural tie-up of the ideas of your essay, nicely brought to a satisfying end, and your essay needs one.

Don't start your closing with, "In closing." That's cheating. It's also the equivalent of starting your introduction with "I deserve this award because" – it's not creative at all. Your closing should speak for itself, without a need to say "in closing" or "listen up, committee, here comes my closing." It's a challenge, but you can do it.

Don't begin your essay with "My name is." Your name should be on the page elsewhere, eliminating any need for you to waste the all-important first sentence of your essay by simply stating your name.

Don't use acronyms without explaining them first. You may know what FBLA or JA or AYBWA is, but that doesn't mean your committee members do. There are hundreds of student organizations out there these days, and not even the most up-to-date scholarship judge is going to know all of them. Spell out the words of the acronym the first time you refer to the organization, and then you can use the acronym from then on.

Use creativity in your writing, but not your format. There are people out there, lots of them, in all fields and walks of life, who will give you a great many variations on this theme: If you want to stand out in life (or break through certain barriers, or win the big contest, or get that big job, etc.), then you've got to be willing to totally shake things up. To do something wild, crazy, nutty, completely unexpected. Such as, say, attending a job interview and belting out a song about why they should hire you, or perhaps walking into that same interview in Bermuda shorts and a neon T-shirt, just to show them that you're a whole different level of creative. Or writing a scholarship essay as a series of haikus, or a Letterman-esque Top Ten List, or in rhyming couplets, etc.

Doing so will definitely get you noticed, in the same way that streaking across center field during a baseball game will get you noticed. But despite the conventional wisdom, not all publicity is good publicity.

Here's the thing about those free-spirited folks who give you such advice, the creative crazies who urge you to burst out of your shell and shock the world with your own unique style: they're usually long gone by the time you actually DO the wacky stuff they've advised you to do. And while your creativity may sometimes be appreciated, often it's not. And even when it is, it may not be appreciated so much that you get the award you're bucking for.

All I mean here is not to turn your essay into something I alluded to earlier: a rhyming poem, a song, a Top 10 Reasons I Should Get This Scholarship List, etc. Sure, I admire the guts it takes to submit such a thing, but a big part of why it takes guts is the knowledge that it's probably going to kill your chances of winning. In terms of scholarship applications, creativity is a means to an end, not the end itself. When in doubt, always remember Rule No. 1: follow instructions!

Send in your essay near the beginning or the end of the application period. Psychological studies indicate that people tend to recall items at the beginning of a list and the end of a list far better than they do those in the middle of the list. Try it yourself --- go look at 20 items in your kitchen, 20 books in your bookcase, or any set of 20 things. Then leave the room, come back, and see which items you remember. You'll certainly remember the very last item or two, because they were the most recent things you saw. And for some reason, you'll remember the first few as well.

Why does it work this way? Beats me, but it works. This is why a highly-touted study method advises you to study in short bursts of an hour at a time and taking frequent breaks, rather than one long period. With many different bursts, there are many different beginnings and endings that stick in your brain, and that increases your total recall.

How does that possibly relate to when you should send in your scholarship essay? Because scholarship judges reading through scholarship essays are the same as you looking through your kitchen items or books, except on a larger scale over a longer period of time (the entire application period). A scholarship judge is much more likely to recall the first few great essays he read and the last few great essays he read than he is to recall some great ones that came along in the middle. This doesn't mean your judge is dumb or forgetful (he may be both, but not on the basis of this phenomenon alone) – it just means he's human. And if there's one point I like to hammer home over and over again in this book, it's that judges are subject to normal human tendencies and you should, where possible, exploit those tendencies.

So when it comes time to send your essay, do so on Day 1 (if you buy the theory that it gives the judges months to soak in how great you are, day after day) or near the end of the application period (if you prefer the recency angle). Either choice leaves you better off than applying in the middle of the application period.

Don't write the same essay for all the scholarships you apply for. Lots and lots of students do this, and you may be one of them. Every now and then, students get the idea that they've written one essay that's so perfect in every way that it can be used to win not only one scholarship, but multiple scholarships. So they submit this essay for each scholarship they find, heedless of the particular requirements of each contest they're entering.

This is generally a very bad idea, for this reason: how likely is it, really, that one essay will even address the specific topics you're required to discuss on different scholarship applications? I suppose there's a small likelihood that a very, very general topic – maybe, "Tell us about yourself" or something equally vague – may be used on more than one scholarship application that you run across. Beyond that, though, it seems unlikely that the same essay will precisely address what different scholarship committees ask you to address. It's easy to spot a cookie-cutter essay, because it usually bears little resemblance to what we've asked for. For example, if our contest asks you to describe how you see yourself in 10 years, and you submit an essay that tells your life story from childhood to the present day but doesn't mention a thing about your future, then we're guessing you're probably carpet-bombing the scholarship world with that essay. Or, as my father would say, throwing a handful of shit at the wall and seeing what sticks. Trust me, nothing will stick.

Don't write or ask the committee or granting institution for advice on how to write your essay. About once a day, someone calls our office asking about our scholarships. "What do you mean by this question?" they ask. "How should I write this? What are you looking for me to say here?"

The answer is always the same: Write it however you like. The company or institution giving the scholarship is going to lay down some guidelines for you in the instructions, but beyond that, it's up to you. Often, there will be some intentional vagueness or, as we prefer to say, "room for interpretation" in those instructions. That's because we want to see how you interpret the question and what road you take to answer it. We can't tell you exactly what to write – it's your job to come up with that on your own.

Show your essay to a teacher who doesn't like you - or at least doesn't know you. Students who actually do go the extra mile and show their essay to a teacher before sending it often go straight to their favorite teacher, or at least one who likes them a lot. That's natural, but if that person is your favorite teacher, then he/she probably likes you, too, and may be likely to pat you on the back and tell you what you want to hear rather than give you the honest feedback your essay needs to improve. This isn't always the case, but it can be, especially with that teacher who seems to want to be good buddies with lots of the students (every school has one). On the other hand, a teacher who doesn't know you (and especially one who does know you and isn't particularly fond of you) doesn't have any reason to lie to you about your essay's shortcomings. In fact, a teacher who doesn't like you may enjoy the opportunity to criticize you. You might as well let him/her do so in a way that helps you out - you could get some very useful feedback from the process. Plus, as an aside, you'll probably earn some respect from that teacher as well. If you know he/she doesn't like you and you still go ask for his/her expertise, that shows guts.

NOTE: I know some of you reading this are thinking something like, "Gosh, I know all the teachers, and I can't even think of ONE teacher who doesn't like me. They all like me!" If that's the case, then - well, good for you. Keep in touch with as many of them as you can for future recommendation letters and references!

Be careful using voice-to-text software. Students rarely do this - for now, it seems to be mostly the domain of the high-level business executive who doesn't like typing. But the technology is beginning to get more sophisticated, and we know that more of you will be using it in the future. Already, we'll occasionally get an essay that a student dictated using the software. How do we know? Sentences like, "I man igsisting student at Statesville Community College." That's not just a misspelling - no one really thinks that's the way to spell "existing" except a computer. You could perhaps chalk this one up under the same category as proofreading and spell-checking, but I gave it its own entry since it's actually a piece of software introducing mistakes that you didn't know about and may not catch unless you pay close attention. Again, however, those are mistakes that another set of eyes reviewing the essay can easily catch.

Chapter VI

Things We Thought Were So Obvious That We Didn't Have To Say Them.

But Apparently We Do.

Do not, under any circumstances, have your parents write essays, letters, or anything else, on your behalf. Over the last few years, the media has been telling us that America is a society where, to be blunt, kids are a lot slower to become independent than they used to be. Apparently it's no big deal to graduate from college and move right back in with your parents for a few more years, often paying no rent. Just like when you were in high school, Mommy has a hot breakfast for you on the table when you roll out of bed at 10 a.m. Except back then, you were actually in school at 10 a.m. Now at 10 a.m., you're halfheartedly cracking open the Classifieds looking for a company who thinks a degree in art history and comparative literature may qualify you for a job. *Fortune* magazine recently ran a story about parents attending job interviews with their children. And I don't mean waiting outside in the lobby; I mean actually sitting next to their sons and daughters at the job interviews themselves. I'm not kidding.

ANYWAY... you can see where we're going with this. Moms and Dads are doing quite a few things for their adult children these days that, not so long ago, were considered to be the jobs of the children themselves. I had always assumed that, despite this disturbing societal shift, all students and parents still knew that scholarship applications were still 100% the responsibility of the student, not the parents. But on a couple of occasions, I have been proven wrong.

I once tore open an envelope to find a two-page (front and back) hand-written letter from the mother of a high-school senior, who made the case for why her daughter should receive our scholarship. Now, I am not a cold-hearted person nor a closed-minded one; I read the entire letter before I made up my mind. When you've read as many thousand scholarship applications as I have, you know there are a lot of strange situations out there that you haven't thought of. Thousands of children are paralyzed and cannot write or type; others are blind, etc. So you have to have an open mind, at least at first.

However, that was not the case here. The mother explained that she'd tried to get her daughter to sit down and do the applications, but that she just couldn't get around to it because of all the other extracurricular activities she was involved with. This is the wrong thing to tell a person who gets hundreds of essays daily, and at all hours of the night, from students who are involved in all those same activities yet still find the time to complete their own scholarship applications without their mothers' help.

Not only that, but the mother's long letter covered very little about her daughter; mostly, it just talked about how badly she needed the money to go to school. I'll always remember that one, obviously – it isn't every day that a mother applies in place of the student – but I also remember it because it was sad. How desperate did that mom have to be in order to pick up a pen and paper and write out a two-page letter, essentially begging for us to send her daughter money?

Do not send your essay with postage due. There are many ways to make a bad first impression, but I can't think of a worse one than making the committee pay money for the privilege of reading your essay. When in doubt, add an extra stamp or two. I hate wasting stamps as much as the next guy, but trust me, you'll never miss that 40 cents.

Do not print your essay in all boldfaced type. Yes, this actually happens, and more than you'd expect. We suspect the writer begins bolding certain passages here and there, and then before long, decides to shoot the moon and bold the whole thing. Don't do it. Bolding text here and there adds emphasis to certain words, setting them apart from the rest, but that's a trick you have to use sparingly or it'll lose its effect. Needless to say, then, when you bold everything, there is no effect at all. Not only that, but the words appear to be screaming at the judges from the paper, and that's not good, either.

Spell everything right. Seriously. No excuses and no exceptions – everything. Here's a little yarn about why it's important to spell things correctly.

My company once managed a very large online events calendar for a major news website in one of the largest cities in the U.S. It was a very important job, but it didn't require a great deal of experience. It was grunt work. So we placed an ad at a local university, looking for an intern to handle the job of editing the calendar. We got dozens of responses, but my favorite one went something like this:

> *Dear Sir:*
>
> *I read with great interest about the job of calender editor with your company. I think I would be an excellent candidate for this job, because I currently work on the events calender for my church, and am very aware of community events and also good with computers. I am excited about the opportunity to become your calender editor and look forward to talking more with you about this opportunity.*
>
> *Sincerely,*
> *Jane Doe*

Maybe I'm biased because I've been a fairly decent speller since I was young, but come on – are you kidding me? The average fifth grader can spell the word "calendar," I guarantee you. And if you can't – hey, get up and walk to one of the walls in your dorm room or apartment. See that big thing with all the squares and numbers on it? Check the cover, and I guarantee you'll see the word "CALENDAR" written somewhere on it. Copy that spelling. That's all you have to do to get it right.

Against my better judgment, I couldn't resist writing this girl back. I don't consider myself to be a crusader for correct spelling, because that's a losing battle if ever there was one. Usually these things just get deleted, but some people are begging for a little correction. And I told myself to feel good about it, because my "tough love" might actually help this girl someday. So I wrote her back, and my response went something like this:

Dear Jane,

Thanks for your inquiry about the calendar job. I wanted to be frank with you and tell you that you were eliminated from consideration for the job due to the fact that you misspelled "calender" three times in your email. To be honest, I couldn't trust you to do error-free work as a calendar editor when you're unable to spell the word "calendar." I wish you the best of luck in the future.

Best regards,

Josh Barsch

I didn't expect her to feel good when she received it, but sometimes you need to hear the unpleasant truth in order to improve, right? Well, not according to Jane. She actually wrote back.

Dear Mr. Barsch,

I don't know why you had to write me back just to tell me about my spelling. I would have liked it better if you had not written me back at all. I am not a perfect speller, but I still think I could have done a very good job.

Sincerely,

Jane Doe

So much for trying to be helpful.

Many people today tend to say that spelling matters less depending on what career you're pursuing. They say things like, "What do you expect? I'm in marketing!" or "I spray for termites. Don't expect me to win the spelling bee." But that's not the point. No one expects you to be a perfect speller or grammarian in your day-to-day life; however, your scholarship application is supposed to be your one-time, absolute best possible effort. It's not just you -- it's you and the dictionary and whoever you can find to proofread it, taking as much time as you need to make this ONE document perfect. Yes, perfect - no errors whatsoever.

Whether you like it or not, if you misspell words on a scholarship application, you are telling the committee that you're lazy, and that's the worst possible thing to tell us. We don't reward laziness with money. We think, "Wow, if this person is putting his/her best foot forward on a scholarship application and it's still this sloppy, how bad does this person's work usually look?"

So how do you get your application into tip-top, error-free shape, even if you can't spell to save your life? For starters, of course, use the spell-check function on your computer program. That will catch most of the obvious errors. But once the document is spell-checked, give a copy of it to friends, teachers, spouse, children or whomever else you know that's a better speller than you are. Ask them straight out, "Would you mind taking two minutes to check my application for mistakes? I'm not a great speller." Not only will you get another set of eyes looking over the application, you're also likely to flatter the person a little. It feels good to have someone acknowledge they respect you enough to seek out your help, doesn't it?

Don't be embarrassed to say you're not a good speller – trust me, you're in good company. Once you've had a few people glance over it for errors, you should have an error-free document. It doesn't take long, and it can make the difference between getting the scholarship and getting your application tossed in the garbage.

Type -- don't handwrite -- your essay. Now that computers are omnipresent, this seems obvious; however, we continue to receive a steady stream of handwritten essays. There are exceptions to this rule: for instance, many of our applicants from Africa and other underdeveloped nations have very limited access to computers, and have no choice but to use paper and pen. But even those applicants are at a disadvantage for one simple reason: legibility. At this point in time, scholarship committees are accustomed to reading typed, laser-printed essays. Even if your handwriting is excellent, it's not as easy to read as a typed essay. So if you absolutely must handwrite – and few people reading these words could make that claim, since you purchased this book over the Internet with a computer! – do so as legibly as you can. But if you can gain access to a computer – even for an hour or so – take your handwritten essay, type it up and print it out.

Do not include sensitive personal information that you're not asked for. In fact, if anyone asks you to submit sensitive information, I'd advise skipping that scholarship altogether, because I know of no reason why a reputable program would be asking for your sensitive personal information.

First, let me clarify what I mean by "sensitive personal information." I'm talking about things like your Social Security number, your driver's license number, bank account information, passwords, logins, etc. I'm not talking about basic contact information like name, physical address, email address, and basic things such as that. After all, if you're lucky enough to actually win the scholarship, the committee needs a way to notify you, and if you don't provide any contact information, you'll never find out you won and you'll never get your money!

Back to the issue of sensitive information: You'd be amazed at how many people enclose their Social Security Number with their essay. I have no idea why that is, nor do I have any idea why a reputable scholarship program would ask for it. If you win a big monetary scholarship, then they may need it for tax purposes later – and if you get to that point, they can ask you after you win. Identity theft is rampant, and a valid SSN is the jackpot for an identity thief, especially if it comes along with the owner's name, address, and other vital information.

Some of our applicants have gone even further. I remember two in particular – one who provided her parents' full tax return (complete with both parents' Social Security numbers, names, addresses, employers, incomes… the whole nine yards), and one gentleman from Africa who included his bank account number.

I'll give both these students the benefit of the doubt and say that SURELY, at one point before sending this info, each paused for at least a moment and thought, "should I really be sending this?" And they likely went ahead and sent the info because of one thing: they trusted the committee not to abuse it. And certainly in our case, they were right to do so. However, mail gets lost, and mail gets stolen. And those who steal mail do it for two reasons: a) to steal money and checks that are in the mail, and b) to steal the personal information within the mail in order to do heavy-duty financial damage later.

Bottom line: Don't send your SSN or any other sensitive information in a scholarship application. Doing so puts you at high risk for little reward.

Don't print your essay on a used piece of paper. Hey, we told you this section was dedicated to the painfully obvious. We wouldn't write about this stuff if it didn't actually happen.

On occasion, we've had essays sent to us that were printed on the back side of personal letters, scratch paper, and other gently-used documents. In one case, the writer scrawled across the back of the essay in pen, "Written on Recycled Paper!" I guess the writer expected the committee to be impressed at her environmentally friendly approach, but it didn't work that way. It just made her look too lazy to find a blank sheet of paper.

Make sure your name is on the essay. Go ahead and laugh, but our committees tell us that about 1 out of every 20-25 essays that we receive has no name on it. And some of them are pretty darn good essays. In fact, I know of at least two times in which committees that I actually served on would've selected no-name essays as winners; obviously, however, we couldn't, since we had no idea who wrote them. Was it you? Probably not, but maybe. You never know.

Even if your essay belongs in the Scholarship Essay Hall of Fame (there should be one of these, shouldn't there? We should start one.), no committee will put any work into tracking down the writer, retracing the envelopes to look for a return address, or anything like that. Your prize-winning words will just get tossed aside and the runner-up will get the money that should've been yours! Ouch! So heed the warning of your third-grade teacher: if your paper has no name, it'll end up in "File 13" – the trash.

Don't use a cursive or novelty font. I debated including this one in the "painfully obvious" section, because hundreds of people have done it over the years, and it's not as indubitably boneheaded as some of the other things in this section, like sending your bank account information or having your mom write your essay for you. But submitting your essay in cursive or novelty font is still a very horrible, never-advisable, avoid-at-all-costs thing to do. Allow me to explain.

Cursive fonts. Here's another of many controversial notions in this book: Cursive is dying. I almost said "dead", but dead means completely extinct, like mastodons; millions of people still write in cursive, of course, most of whom are over 50 years old. I mean that cursive is dying in the same way other once-omnipresent things without anyone to carry on their torch are dying: newspapers, American Indian languages, workplace smoking, and the like. None of them are quite dead yet, but it's just a matter of borrowed time and everybody knows it.

Cursive used to be considered the "grown-up" way to write. You learned it in the third or fourth grade, and it was expected to be your sole form of written communication by the sixth grade. And just before you left the sixth grade, your teacher would issue a not-so-veiled threat to the entire class: "When you get to junior high, you must write everything in cursive. If you turn in a paper that's not in cursive, they just throw it right into the garbage." Then you got to junior high and found out it was all a lie. They were just beating cursive into your head for... well, for no apparent reason. Just because their teachers had done the same thing to them decades ago, with a good paddling thrown in here and there for good measure.

This was long before the personal computer, in a time when no one imagined that computers would ever be affordable enough for everyone to have one and long before the convenience of email would force the entire population to use keyboards. So when you put those two things together: 1) everyone has a computer, and 2) everyone wants to use email instead of write letters, you get 3) no need for cursive. Personally, I think that 50 years from now, the ability to read cursive will be akin to the ability to read Braille or hieroglyphics. They will all be equally foreign to the average reader of English.

So, how does this relate to your scholarship essay? It simply means that going out of your way to use a cursive or script font (fun fact of the day: in cursive fonts, the letters actually touch each other; in script fonts, they don't), you're actually making your document more difficult to read.

Novelty fonts. Using novelty fonts is a sin more grave, even, than using cursive fonts. At least cursive used to be considered the fancy, sophisticated way to write. Novelty fonts, on the other hand, have always been for novelty only. That's why they're called novelty fonts, people. There's plenty of room for creativity in the content of your essay, but don't insert much creativity into your font selection. Have you enjoyed reading this paragraph so far? Of course you haven't. It's been a little slower going than reading the rest of this book, now hasn't it? Now, imagine trying to read an entire scholarship essay written in this font. Not fun. OK, I'm going to change fonts now. You ready for me to change fonts? Are you sure? How about now? OK, I'm really going to change fonts now.

Readability is key (and if reading the above paragraph didn't prove that to you, nothing will!), so stick with time-tested serif fonts like Times, Times New Roman or Palatino, or sans serifs such as Arial, Helvetica, or Verdana, maybe even Tahoma. Don't even think about a novelty font: it may make your essay memorable, but only for the annoyance it caused by being so difficult to read.

Don't use novelty envelopes or paper. I've already covered the type of paper and envelopes you should use for your application, so if you've read this far, you can consider this a review. Just so we're clear, though: you should save the Hello Kitty envelopes and sparkly pink paper – or the NASCAR stationery with "In Loving Memory of #3" envelopes -- for personal correspondence.

Don't trash-talk the committee. Back when we were switching our scholarship over from postal mail to e-mail, I made a joke on one of our websites about the U.S. Postal Service. I know, I know – you're thinking, "That's impossible! How could you possibly find something negative to say about the U.S. Postal Service?" I don't remember exactly what it was that I said, but I know it wasn't cruel or spiteful – it went something like, "there's no reason to line the pockets of the USPS anymore, because we're now accepting submissions only via email." If you've read this far, you already know that I have little love in my heart for the USPS, so I think I did pretty well by restricting my comments to just that.

I mean, really, it could've been a lot worse. I didn't mention their propensity to lose and destroy mail and never lift a finger to take responsibility or offer compensation for it. I didn't mention that they hike stamp prices more often that the rest of us hike up our pants. I didn't mention that you can stand in line at a U.S. Post Office longer than some kids stand in line to get a PlayStation 3, and I didn't mention that the customer service skills make the Department of Motor Vehicles look like the Ritz-Carlton. And last but not least, I didn't mention that every couple of years, one unlucky post office becomes a shooting gallery after a nutso package-sorter brings an assault rifle to work and decides to play a real-life version of Metal Gear Solid with anyone who comes into his field of vision.

A week or so later, we got a nasty email from a high school senior who insisted that she was certain she was qualified to win our scholarship - but refused to enter due to our "alarming and insensitive" comments about the post office.

Her letter left me with several observations: 1) Who loves the United States Postal Service so much that they would both write a letter of outrage about such an innocuous comment, and refuse to enter our scholarship contest in protest of that comment? Maybe both her parents were mail carriers. 2) If you thought that was alarming and insensitive, then you'd better not read what I just wrote in "Confessions of a Scholarship Judge," because that might just give you a heart attack; 3) Good, don't apply. That's one more essay I don't have to read before I go home and play with my children; 4) I actually feel a little bit sorry for her. If she really was "alarmed" by the post office crack, then she is in for a very rough go in this crazy, unpredictable world.

The moral of the story is this (yes, there's actually a lesson here, not just an excuse for me to rant): Don't waste your time lecturing the committee. Trust me, they'll get plenty of good applicants with or without yours. If you don't enter, no one will care or even notice. Except maybe your parents, who will have to dig into their savings to pay your college the money that you could've won with the scholarship.

Don't plagiarize other people's work. The Internet has made it easier than ever to pass off the work of others as your own, but if you're bold enough to do so, beware of the double-edged sword: the Web also makes it easier than ever to catch you in the act. A stolen essay can be uncovered often and easily by Googling any sentence or phrase that sounds like it may have been lifted. An exact-phrase search on Google will often uncover the original source, which will, of course, expose any plagiarism immediately. And if we've got a good gut feeling that a paper has been plagiarized, then we won't just Google a phrase or two; we'll Google 15 or 20. A crafty plagiarist knows this strategy and will take measures to neutralize it by changing the wording of certain sentences. But they won't go to the trouble of changing them all, and therein lies the likelihood they'll get caught. After all, cheaters cheat to get out of doing the work that the rest of us do. If you were willing to go to the trouble of altering every sentence of an essay, you probably aren't nearly as lazy as most cheaters!

Honestly, I doubt this is a problem for anyone reading this book. If you paid good money for Confessions because you want to learn how to earn more scholarship money, you're not the type of loser who plagiarizes.

Chapter VII

Parting Shots

You didn't think this book was going to end without a conclusion, did you? No way, Jose. There's far too much information in Confessions and GiveMeScholarships.com to just stop on a dime, without a little bit of a wrap-up.

First things first, though: While you may have arrived at the end of this book, your relationship with the GiveMeScholarships.com team is just beginning. This is a lifetime product, and as such, you'll be hearing from us every few months, indefinitely, in the form of updates to this book, podcasts, newsletters, and whatever we think might help you win more scholarships. We'll send you updates via email, and we'll use the email address you gave us when you bought Confessions. If you'd like us to send your updates to a different email address, just drop us a line at help@givemescholarship.com and we'll update your address.

There's a lot of information to digest in this book, so if your head is swimming, don't worry. It takes a while for it all to sink in, and it takes practice to master a lot of the items that we've covered. You're not going to wake up tomorrow doing everything perfectly right, so don't place those expectations on yourself.

However, here's what you can do: keep improving, little by little, every time you submit a scholarship application. Every time you write an essay, pull out this book and check yourself against the items we've presented here. Did you print that essay on high-quality paper, and did you put it in a glossy folder and a full-sized envelope? Those items are easy and quick to master. Did you use a lot of redundant language? Were your transitions good? Were your introductions and closings as creative as you could make them? Those may take a little longer to get down.

But hang in there and keep giving it your best effort, because there's simply too much money out there for the taking for you to do anything else. College is more expensive than ever, and scholarships you win can change your life. The bigger the scholarship you win, the bigger the change in your life. Don't believe me? Then check this out:

If you can pull off a $5,000 scholarship, that's $5,000 in student loans that you don't have to take out. And that means 10 years – 10 entire years! – of paying $100 or so per month, every single month. Instead of paying that money to the government in the form of student loan repayment, you could sock away $12,000 or so for your retirement. And assuming a modest 8 percent rate of appreciation, that $12,000 can easily grow to over $120,000 in 30 years! In 40 years, it'll grow to over $260,000! **Now do you believe that one scholarship can change your life forever?**

That's exactly why we take this scholarship stuff as seriously as we do: it's serious, life-changing business. It's as simple as that. And I hope you'll put this book to the best possible use and score yourself a big scholarship and a corresponding life change like the one I've described above.

In the meanwhile, rest assured that while you're working hard on your upcoming scholarship deadlines, the GMS team is working hard on your next update. If you've got any questions, comments, requests, or anything else you might like to see in the next update or simply something you think we should know, drop us a line at help@givemescholarships.com. Until then, we wish you the best of luck in your scholarship hunt. Keep putting that Best Foot Forward, ok?

Yours in Success,

Josh Barsch

Appendix

Outstanding, Real-Life Essays
with commentary in bold by Josh Barsch

How to Use This Appendix

This book is so full of "do this" and "don't do this" advice that you may just be left with the impression that we never receive any essays we like. Nothing could be further from the truth! We get great essays all the time; they're just the minority.

The following folks have agreed to let us use their essays as examples of the stuff we like to see from applicants. They encompass a wide variety of disciplines and writing styles. All of them illustrate one or more pieces of advice that you've read in the Book, and I've marked my commentary in red letters so that you'll easily be able to tell when it's me talking or the author talking.

I've included these essays so that you'll have some real-life examples to illustrate the points I make elsewhere in the Book. I can say "do this" and "don't do this" all day long, but sometimes you just need some examples so that it all makes sense. For instance, I can tell you that you need to write a good introduction and conclusion, but that's not nearly as helpful as having some concrete examples of these principles done well.

So enjoy these sample essays, and I thank the contributors very much for allowing their inclusion in the Book. If you have any questions or comments about these essays, feel free to ask them on the GMS blog at http://www.GiveMeScholarships.com or email us at info@givemescholarships.com. Thanks, and good luck!

Yours in Success,

Josh Barsch

CEO, GiveMeScholarships.com

Sophia Pierre

Dreams are what make life worth living. **(Simple, but powerful. I like it.)** They motivate you to work hard and to stand strong during trials and tribulations. The great thing about them is that there is not just one uniform way of achieving them. Everybody has their own way of achieving their dreams. My way is classic. I seek to fulfill my dreams through pursuing a post secondary education. Getting a chance to go to college is in itself a dream come true for me. **(OK, I'm intrigued...why is that a "dream come true"? Let's see...)**

The day I realized that I wanted to pursue a post-secondary education is the day my mom shared with me that she grew up poor in Haiti. I was sixteen years old at the time and it was an ordinary day. My mother was yelling at me to clean my room because it was so messy that you couldn't see the floor. I didn't have the energy to do it but I knew that it had to be done or I wouldn't see the outside of my house for a while. (funny!) So I started by getting rid of things that I felt were of no value to me anymore like shoes, clothes, and old socks. While I was in the middle of doing so, my mother walked in to check on my progress. She saw the things that I was throwing away and asked me very sternly why I was getting rid of them. I didn't understand why she was taking that tone with me because after all I was just doing what she asked me to do. She picked up one of the shoes and said, "You kids do not appreciate what you have, nor do you understand what you are throwing away." I sensed something in her voice, like she was about to cry. **(I can see it coming here, a story about her mother growing up poor in Haiti. I like how this is set up... a girl is innocuously cleaning up her room of what she considers "clutter" and unwittingly unlocks strong memories from her mother)** I didn't understand where all this sorrow was coming from but I guessed she read the puzzled look on my face and began to tell me her story.

When my mother was growing up, her family was way below the poverty line. My grandmother didn't know how to read or write because her parents couldn't afford to send her to school. So she did odd jobs here and there in order to support her five children. When my grandmother went off to work, it was my mother who took care of the youngsters. Due to malnutrition and disease, two of my mother's siblings died. They lived in what my mother calls a box. There weren't any beds; they all slept on the floor huddled close. **(This is a gruesome portrait... simply written but written well)**. My grandmother could barely afford to send my mother to school, but she managed to do so by doing without some necessities like nice clothes and comfortable shoes **(hence, her mother's reaction to her daughter's attempt to throw away perfectly good shoes and socks)**. My mother was teased for being so poor because back then, to dream of escaping such poverty was too far fetched. But that dream came true for them when my Aunt who made it in America sent for the rest of the family back in Haiti. Once she arrived in America, my mother wasted no time turning a new leaf and worked to become a successful woman.

That day I had a lot of firsts. It was the first time I saw my mother cry. It was the first time I learned about my mother's past. It was the first time I learned I would have had two other uncles. Most importantly, it was the first time that I seriously started to think about my life and where I wanted to be twenty years from then. It was the first time I decided that even though I had some odds against me -- for instance, my race and my gender -- judging by my mother's situation, success wasn't impossible. **(I like how immediate assumption of gender/racial bias is immediately followed up with the assertion that success is indeed possible, regardless).** My mother made it, so I realized that success wasn't a dream too far fetched for me. I decided that in order to achieve that dream, I had to pursue a higher education by going to a college that would prepare me for the outside world. As for the things I was throwing away, I gave them to my grandmother so she could give them away when she went back to Haiti **(Good job bringing this full circle!).** I figured my trash would be somebody else's treasure. Like the things I was going to throw away, I decided not to throw away my chances of being successful one day.

(Overall, an interesting brief story about how what could've been just an innocent room-cleaning turned into a young woman's awakening about the possibilities that lie ahead. Great!)

But with success come trials and tribulations. When I first started at Northeastern, I didn't think I was going to make it past the first year. Northeastern is so expensive, and the financial aid barely covers half. I have to commute for an hour everyday to get to school because I can't afford to live in the dorms. In the beginning, my mother was the only one paying for my tuition, and by the grace of God I am still here. But it seems that as each year goes by, money gets tighter and things get harder. **(The committee identifies with this, very much.)** This in part is due to the fact that my mother decided to go back to school to pursue her nursing career. Next to buying a house, finishing nursing school is one of her biggest dreams. She had to put her career on hold because she had my older sister who was diagnosed with Type I Diabetes. As a baby I was diagnosed with lead poisoning and was hospitalized. To make matters worse, my father was not very supportive and abusive at times. So my mother packed up and left, knowing that what lie ahead was a rough road as a single mother.

Now that my sister and I are older, my mom has decided to reopen that chapter in her life that she never got to finish, and I support her all the way **(It's a good idea to add this, so we know you're supportive and not resentful for the additional difficulty it's caused).** But it's like a double-edged sword. In order to finish what she has started, we have had to make a lot of sacrifices. In order to attend school my mother has cut her hours at work, which cuts her check in half and makes it hard for her to make ends meet. She is barely able to keep up with all the bills, and she is no longer able to help me pay for school. For the past year, I have been paying for my tuition, with some help from my father and divine intervention **(I would've liked to hear more about this "divine intervention").** However, I recently was laid off of my job of almost four years. That job was my safety net because I was able to pay tuition, buy books, and help with some of the living expenses. I had to go on unemployment for 2 months before I was able to get another job and get back on my feet. The job that I have now doesn't pay me nearly as well as my last job did, so I must resort to other means of funding, which is why I chose to apply for this scholarship. Every little bit of help counts.

Things are hard, but I have faith they will get better. Sometimes I worry because I feel so close to getting my degree, yet so far because I always have to think about where the money is coming from to pay for tuition. I can't enjoy just being a college student because the tuition is always in the back of my mind. But God always finds a way for me to get through another year. The struggle is hard, but it makes the reward that much sweeter. When things seem hopeless, I keep in mind and in my heart a verse from the Bible, James 1:2-14":

"Consider it pure joy, my brothers, whenever you face trials of many kinds, because you know that the testing of your faith develops perseverance....Blessed is the man who perseveres under trials, because when he has stood the test, he receives the crown of life that God has promised to those who love him."

(Despite my warning not to make religion the core of one's scholarship essay, I have no problem at all with quoting a Bible verse that gives you strength.)

Every year that passes shows my perseverance and my dedication to pursuing my dreams, despite the odds. You can't get something for nothing; therefore I plan to give my all. So far, God has helped me through three years of school, and he will be by my side for the last two. **(I take this as an assurance to the committee that Sophia will make it** through college regardless of any obstacles she faces, and that is exactly the type of person we enjoy rewarding with scholarship money).

Once I finish school and receive my degree, I plan on entering the media field. I've always wanted to be involved in media and the entertainment industry, which is why I decided to major in communications (I also have a Business Administration minor). With the ability to be omnipresent, the media has the power to penetrate the mind, affect train of thought, and shape self-perception **(interesting choice of words, all of them true)**. Media outlets are supposed to provide entertainment as well as pertinent information to the public. Overall the media is supposed to provides a means for expression. However, I feel that the media has taken on the role of defining this idea of the ideal image by displaying images on magazines covers and on television screens that do not portray the average woman. The media looks like hypocrites, because even though it is an outlet for one to take advantage of their first amendment rights, this idea of the "ideal" goes against individual expression (another interesting take on the media. Warning: "media" is a plural noun, not a singular noun, so the verb should be "looks" instead of "look"). This especially affects (the correct usage of "affect"!) teenage girls because they are not going to take the time to realize that the perfect images on the magazine covers have been digitally rebuffed to hide imperfections, or the work it takes behind the scenes to make an individual look like a million bucks on camera. A significant decrease in the self-esteem among teenage girls today is the result of constant exposure to media content that glorify ideal representations of true beauty. **(All good points, very likely to resonate with the committee)**

To achieve this "ideal", the anorexia and bulimia rate are rising **(where's the support for this statement?)**, and there exists a color gap in the minority community **(I don't know what this means)**.Some girls are not capable of achieving this ideal look, and when they come to this realization, they could possible succumb to depression or turn to self-mutilation. This issue is close to my heart because I understand the pressure to fit the ideal, and coping with the reality of not being able to ever do that. I have friends who have dealt with depression and anorexia as a result of low self-esteem. Depression is an issue I dealt with my whole freshman year of high school. I want to be in the forefront of the production of media content so I could help produce material that embraces individuality and acceptance of self. I want magazines to not only show the beauty of size one but also the beauty in size ten or sixteen. I also want to help create an outlet where the unseen is seen.

Too many shows focus on the rich and famous. **(I agree wholeheartedly. Noble aspirations here).**

There are not enough programs that focus on common everyday people. Overall, I want to see to it that the promise for freedom of speech, expression, and individualism is actually delivered.

I don't only see a degree as a desire, but a need. I need to get a degree so I could give back to those who have helped me the most, which are my family and my African American forefathers and mothers **(Martin Luther King, Malcolm X, etc)** who paved the way and made it possible for me to go to school. For me to not take advantage of this opportunity would seem like an injustice.

I'd rather be the person that someone could lean on instead of the person who does the leaning. I'd rather be the person who gives instead of the person doing the taking. I don't want to dread waking up early in the morning to get ready for a job that I hate. **(You've got that right, Sophia)** I want to look forward to the day ahead because I know that somehow I am making a difference and contributing to something. A degree opens so many doors to me, and I am assured that when one door closes another will open. With a degree in hand, the possibilities are endless!

(Overall, I like it very much. She told a good story and transitioned well over to what her aspirationsare, and shared some very unique and inspirational thoughts. A very strong essay.)

Aaron Bregman

Growing, Learning and Teaching

The idea of being a teacher is daunting. Teachers are credited with touching lives, molding students' interests, raising generations and helping to formulate new ideas. Learning about the pros and cons of teaching, the system, and what makes a good teacher was initially intimidating to me. I would sit through class thinking to myself that a 21-year-old college boy who loves to watch baseball and talk about the Teenage Mutant Ninja Turtles has no right getting inside the head of a seventeen-year-old student. **(Hilarious! All of us who teach feel that way at some time.)** That I would have no right teaching a child about the wonders of democracy, the beauty of American history, the intricate nature of English grammar or the complications of quantum physics. However, upon more careful consideration it became clear that the tricks to being a good student are equivalent to the tricks of being a good teacher. Throughout my career as a student, I have had the opportunity to lead clubs, to counsel younger children, and to gain a sense of appreciation for knowledge at its most basic state. These experiences allow me to understand the different multi-intelligence theories of all age groups. These experiences and realizations are priceless, and universal.

Human nature dictates that as an individual grows, learns, and experiences the world, they will start to develop a fervor or enthusiastic craze for a particular subject or topic. For example, many Americans take pride and passion in their various communal organizations and clubs. They find fulfillment in helping to build a vibrant, meaningful and successful community. However, while the ends justify the means, the life of a communal leader, or club president is frequently a demanding one (This is a wise observation). I learned this through my high school tenure as president of my local youth group chapter, and through being the president of the Jewish Students Association at American University. I learned that holding a position of such magnitude means that people expect you to take yourself and the community seriously (You got it. Another good observation). It's hard work, long hours and at times, people become difficult to deal with. Time management, programming, and inter-personal relationships are nearly impossible to manage. However, when I am able to balance the three, the reward is incredible. The satisfaction from being able to relate to my peers, and create programs that will help them reach out to one another, and help them to discover themselves is priceless. After each successful program, I feel as if I have changed the world by changing one life.

(This paragraph reflects a lot of maturity. Many writers talk about wanting to save the world, but few realize the demands that come along with such dreams and the necessity of keeping it all in balance.)

I know that that very feeling is the same one that I am going to experience in the near future as I stand in front of a class, eager to learn, eager to explore their relationship with texts, with concepts, with group work, and with me. I know that my students will become difficult to deal with—arguing about unfair grades, creating an extraordinary amount of fantastic excuses to justify their lack of timely homework assignments. The hours of being a teacher are difficult as well. Waking up early, working straight through the day, just to return home to write lesson plans and grade papers seems almost not worth the effort. However, the gratification will not come from the sleep, or the paychecks, but will come from knowing that I made a difference in the life of a child, that I opened him or her up to a new idea or concept. I know that I will be just as passionate about making my lesson plans work as I am about making my programming work. To teach is to touch a life. **(The "touch a life" and "touching the life of a child" are borderline clichés, but I give you a pass because I can tell you truly mean what you say.)**

In addition to spending my academic years working with different clubs and organizations, I spend my summers working with children at a day camp. My camp director once taught me, that being a camp counselor requires more than just managerial skills. Of course it is fun being in the sun all day, being able to swim, and bonding with co-counselors, but that "summer dream" aspect of the job vanishes quickly when one out of fifteen campers is horsing around and gets hurt falling down on the basketball court. The philosophy behind being a good counselor is that your number one priority is to ensure the physical and emotional well being of the campers while being a good role model. However, every now and then, counselors do occasionally need to be reminded that while camp is fun, it is a job. The desire to be a camp counselor stems from my fantastic experiences as a camper. I feel it my responsibility to give back to the younger generation to show them what was given to me as a camper. Helping campers growing by using their kinesthetic intelligence, I want to create a camp environment that runs smoothly, and creates growth and successful opportunities for children in the places they would be likely to find them; on the basketball court, in the pool, or in arts and crafts.

In a lot of respects, being a teacher is just a more "cleaned up" version of being a camp counselor. It is just as difficult to manage twenty-five chatty teenagers, as it is to manage fifteen hyperactive five year olds. **(Probably more so!)** The general concept is the same; both thirst for attention, for successful opportunities. While campers look for these opportunities in obvious mediums—like sports and competitions, educational success is a little trickier. It is certain that students look for success and justification through grades, but there is so much more to education. My job as a teacher goes beyond the physical traits of hard work through deciding a grade (which is little, if anything, more than a squiggle on a piece of paper). **(Somebody's been reading his Confessions book about the relevance of GPA...)**

However, I must create success and growth opportunities for them through exciting lesson plans, where they can create and show off to each other in a fun and academic setting. I must also be an intellectual role model for my students, teaching them that it is cool to being able to understand Shakespeare, or teach them that it is not dorky to know all fifty states in alphabetical order. By being a teacher, I will need to teach my students about general literacy, but more than that, I will teach them what it means to be a human being.

By being a good student now, fortunate enough to share my education with fantastic professors in college, I am on convinced that I too will make a good teacher. The teachers I have had the opportunity to study with have gone out of heir way in order to teach me to grow up. I have learned valuable facts and morals from a variety of textbooks and novels. I an calculate my tax and tip when I go out to dinner. I can watch the news and analyze the situations between the bias journalistic words and between the real facts that took place. I know what I wanted to learn as a student, and I am excited to give to the younger generations what I have always craved. I have learned that boring lectures, with long unnecessary vocabulary words are a waste of everyone's time, so I can't wait to find mediums of art, role-play, and music to express my lessons. I know that I am going to treat my students, as I have always wanted to be treated—with respect, with faith, and with dedication. I was never given up on by the system or by my teachers, and I have no intent of giving up on it.

It is really incredible to sit back and think about the fact that through nothing more than life experiences I feel confident to teach others. Each experience I have lived has taught me something that I am yearning to teach. Time management, community relations, creating opportunities, seeing the big picture, and realizing the fundamental value of education for education's sake have been the most paramount keystones of my young adult life. I hope to continue to learn, to continue to grow, and to continue to feed off of my teachers and my environment.

A very wise, mature essay written in a very down-to-earth style. Worthy of emulation.

Aimee Fay

In the fall of 2007, I will attend Antioch University in Seattle to complete the last two years of my liberal arts bachelor's degree. I am planning to then attend the master's program in occupational therapy (OT) at University of Puget Sound in Tacoma. Much research and reflection has gone into these choices. **(Not creative, but straight and to the point, that's for sure. Not a word wasted, which I can appreciate)**

To fulfill pre-requisite requirements for my master's program, Antioch is my first choice for its emphasis on psychology, teaching, and art-therapy. This curricula is a strong and specific foundation for my graduate studies and career; furthermore I am in the process of designing my own degree program in Somatic Psychology, an option that is available exclusively at Antioch **(designing your own degree program is pretty impressive)**. Although I recognize that a private school is a more expensive alternative in the immediate financial sense, I think it is worth the extra burden. The school also allows me to receive credit for prior-learning experience and for volunteer work at hospitals and clinics that I plan to do while attending Antioch in reparation for my master's program.

After visiting and researching the two possible schools in the area for master's work in OT, I am even more confident of my school and career choices. After attending an open house at University of Washington's program and speaking extensively with students and staff there, I then visited the University of Puget Sound and met with their program director, OT admissions staff and students. I felt that again, even though the price is higher financially that I would be getting my money's worth by the insurance I received in investing in an educational environment that best fits my learning style. The campus is peaceful and full of trees and the people were less hurried **(I don't like this sentence; trees don't translate into a particular learning style, and it's tough to judge the general hurriedness on one visit!)**. Moreover, I like the school's focus on individual investigation and independent research which will allow me to investigate more specific directions within the discipline. **(This, however, definitely speaks to the learning environment, and as a judge, it makes up for the last sentence that I didn't like)**

Finally, I also will benefit by Antioch's close proximity to my home and my son's school. This scholarship will help me to attend school full-time while balancing the responsibilities of single parenting and homework. It is a priority of mine to continue to support my son in his education while at the same time pursuing my own educational aspirations. **(A very noble thing that impresses the committee)**

For over twelve years, I have juggled being a single mother, a massage therapist, a yoga teacher and a student. All these occupations have taught me much about health, balance and about how similar the various disciplines of medicine and art really are. In fact the most essential task of all medical professionals is to guide, facilitate and support the process of self-responsibility in each individual. The most effective way to do this is through respecting each of the patient's own inherent and creative healing processes.

I believe this attitude of cooperation and working holistically with each patient rather than prescribing treatments for generic diseases will be a valuable contribution to the medical world/community, and it is what draws me to the career of occupational therapy. Occupational therapy, and its inherently patient-centered approach, allows more broad and creative thinking than most modern health professions **(I'm taking your word for it here, because I don't know this about OT)**. Thankfully, an important emerging trend in medicine in general is to lean back toward these ancient roots of encouragement of individualized self-healing. One of these traditions is Ayurveda, a "sister science" to yoga. Originally yoga teachers practiced this form of medicine and also Vedic astrology as part of their profession.

In Ayurvedic philosophy, doctors are trained to look first at the "excellences" of a patient, thereby availing themselves of the deepest medicinal tools and remedies possible: the patient's own particular strengths. If a person comes to the Ayurvedic doctor with a certain complaint, no matter how specific that complaint, the first principle is to recognize the patient's strengths (and to help illuminate these strengths for the patient rather than keep their medicine secret). For example, if the doctor notices the fine quality of the patient's voice or love of singing, they suggest chanting exercises that will help build confidence, joy and a stronger immune system. If a person seems very kind, the doctor suggests public service with special attention to personal boundaries and self-care. If they like to dance or move their body, the doctor may suggest yoga postures that balance their level of activity, an so forth. **(A very good, clear explanation of Ayurvedic philosophy, which I knew nothing about until reading this essay)**

My favorite instance of this situation-specific approach is in a story that my yoga teacher in India's son, Kausthub, a yoga teacher himself, told. He works primarily with children with physical disabilities and/or behavioral problems.

A little girl, a six-year old daughter of very successful and busy parents came to Kausthub as a student, her parents hoping to "cure her excessive selfishness". Weeks of therapy went by and she began to trust her new teacher. One day he sent her home with a goldfish in a bowl. The parents were furious. Why did you do such a presumptuous thing, they asked Kausthub. "We don't have time to care for this pet. You know that." Somehow Kausthub convinced them to let the daughter have a chance to care for the fish. And she did. The parents found the results of this action baffling. The little girl quite rapidly began to change temperament. Kausthub's plan worked – giving the child something to care for and a response to her need of relationship was therapeutic. Building trust for her teacher and loving attention of someone honoring her needs for self-healing in the most basic way, gave her enough support that she did not need to protest her perceived neglect so loudly and even more importantly, she began to build relationships in the world around her.

I expect that this little girl, just as all humans do, continued to have challenges. The important thing is that she had an experience of positive support in her life. This support is what I am interested in practicing and encouraging in my occupational therapy patients. **(Here again is a wise observation that we don't see often; the dual acknowledgement that there aren't quick fixes to all of life's problems, but also that alternative ways of seeing the world can begin to scratch away at those problems. I specifically address this in "Confessions," and Aimee gives a perfect example here)**

Creative self-healing within healthy relationship has been an essential part of my teaching yoga at Seattle Central. This is what Kausthub, his family and teachers of this lineage have taught me. Of Krishnamacharya, Kausthub's grandfather and teacher, magazine writer Fernando Pages Ruiz said:

While he had enormous respect for the past, he also didn't hesitate to experiment and innovate. By developing and refining different approaches, he made yoga accessible to millions.

That, in the end is his greatest legacy. As diverse as the practices in Krishnamacharya's different lineages have become, passion and faith in yoga remain their common heritage. The tacit message his teaching provides is that yoga is not a static tradition: it is a living, breathing art that grows constantly through each practitioner's experiments and deepening experience. **(You can really feel her passion for the subject matter here, can't you? Personally, I am not into yoga one bit and I don't empathize with what she's saying, but that doesn't diminish for me her passion for the subject, which makes the essay strong)**

At Seattle Central, I have benefited greatly from knowledge and practice of this originally-intended perspective of yoga as a living, breathing art. After eight years of teaching at the college, I attended a two-year therapeutic yoga teacher training in this philosophy of Krishnamacharya's tradition. We focused specifically on one-on-one adaptations for students of all abilities. Seattle Central has been a great place for me to begin experimentation with these individualized adaptations. Whenever I have found myself tempted to homogenize students, the students have ultimately been my teacher in what works best for them and it is not always what I expect. For instance, one student was in my class for almost two months before we ever talked much individually. He was very busy with his job and family. Every time I would look at him in class he was doing his own movements that seemed not to have much to do with what I directed as a teacher. I was honestly wondering about his apparent lack of nervous system ability. This went on for many weeks, until he approached me one day after class and said very respectfully, "I want you to know that I don't mean to insult your instruction. I just find this the only place that I can do the accident-rehabilitation exercises that my physical therapist prescribed." I didn't know how to respond. Was he fulfilling class requirements? Was he learning anything about yoga? I just said, "Thank you very much for telling me that." I thought about this student's bold choices for many days and nights and finally decided that there is no one way to learn yoga and that he was fulfilling the requirements of the class which were to show up and to get out of the class what he put into it. I had pledged to give my students the benefit of the doubt that they were doing their best. I had not expected this variation of participation. This student (and others) left me with an even deeper interest in the role of the patient's creativity in their own healing and how this is best encouraged. **(Sign of maturity here: admitting you don't know all the answers and acknowledging that much can be learned from the world around you.)**

I plan to practice these same principles of respect and cooperation that I have learned from teaching in my career as an occupational therapist. The philosophies and practices of the two fields are very compatible as inspirations for self-responsibility in the literal sense of the word – the ability to respond. This ability to respond is the key to creating a cooperative and consensual plan for rehabilitation. Occupational therapy itself is a collaborative effort between healthcare practitioners working with the patient and one another. In order to augment this therapeutic cooperation, I am looking forward to integrating the ancient wisdom of Yoga with the dynamic, "living, breathing art" of medicine.

(A great closing that ties up Aimee's future plans as an occupational therapist with her current passion for yoga and all of the philosophies that go with it. Well done!)

Ryan Koons

It was the Sunday before 'Common Ground on the Hill' and it was a crazy time. Volunteers running to the airport to pick up teachers and students, attendees who were unfamiliar with the campus trying to find their rooms, old friends seeing each other for the first time in a year, everyone meeting new people, someone suddenly realizing that their guitar was sitting on their bed, on the next continent - a mass of organized confusion.

(A great brief introduction here. I don't know what "Common Ground on the Hill" is, and Ryan knows that I don't know, but I'm still intrigued about it. It sounds exciting to me.)

I was trying to organize my stage crew and to figure out what I needed them to do. I had requested that my volunteers get to the stage an hour early, and somehow we got everything prepared for the night's events on time.

It was now early evening, and the start of student orientation. The director of Common Ground traditionally starts each orientation with the same song; the lyrics are: 'Hello stranger. Put your loving hand in mine. Hello stranger. Put your loving hand in mine. You are a stranger, but you're a friend of mine.'

The melody is extremely simple, and he sang only three verses. But before it was over, everyone was singing along. People who had met each other only 10 minutes before were brought together over this simple melody with its extremely powerful message.

After the orientation, I was breaking down the stage and getting to know my stage crew, when, out of the corner of my eye, I saw a group of musicians who had met that evening start to play traditional music together. When I was ready to leave campus at midnight, the jam session was still going strong. it would probably last until at least two in the morning. I went home and tried to sleep, but the joy I got from the multi-cultural experience was too strong.

(A tad too long of an intro for my taste, but the story was set up nicely, start to finish)

Common Ground on the Hill is a traditional arts gathering. Instructors teach classes at McDaniel College in Westminster, Md., for two weeks every summer, and artists gather at an arts festival hosted on the weekend between the two weeks of classes. People come from all over the world to teach the traditions of their cultures.

I have been involved in it since it began in 1994, more heavily so for the last couple of years. I started volunteering as a member of the 'Hospitality Suite' when I was in middle school. I helped teachers and students find their classes, ran papers to the copy center for instructors, helped to move heavy instruments from point A to point B, and did a multitude of small errands. I was mingling with some of the biggest names in traditional music, but I did not know this at the time. I only knew Bill Spence, one of the revivers of the Hammered Dulcimer, as the nice guy with the heavy instrument, and the traditional Celtic group Craobh Rua, from Northern Ireland, as the group whose concert went way past my bedtime. During my breaks, I sat in on classes as diverse as Native American Philosophy and Bluegrass Fiddling. I soon began to realize something special was happening in what is basically my backyard. The campus is not fifteen minutes from our house. I was soon hooked. The older I became, the more involved I wanted to become. **(Fascinating. Very attention-grabbing, unique stuff you're writing about here)**

Common Ground 2000 brought an excellent tin whistle player from Scotland named Wattie Lees. My dad had been playing tin whistle in our family-based Celtic Ensemble for years, and I myself had picked up the instrument recently. My dad and I took the class together, and I really enjoyed it and learned a lot from Wattie. The following year, I took a Scottish fiddling class and became more interested in traditional music from the Celtic lands. My involvement with Common Ground escalated, until this past summer when I served as Stage Manager, with several stages and an entire stage crew to organize. It was my job to schedule the stage crew and make sure performers and sound staff had everything they needed during the concerts. I have never enjoyed such an experience as much as I did this one. As stage manager I got to work with diverse musicians and learn from them in the process.

It was this past year's Common Ground that really helped me to decide my major for college: ethnomusicology- the study and preservation of ethnic music. It really opened my eyes this past summer when I realized that I already am an ethnomusicologist: I perform traditional Celtic music regionally with Wherligig, our family-based musical quartet. I also preserve tunes through a music notation program so they can be played and enjoyed in the future, and I have a ravenous interest in the traditional ethnic music of different cultures. It is an interest I want to cultivate and expand. **(Again, very interesting and unique. Clearly, Ryan's passion is coming through loud and clear, as is his dedication to the culture he's describing)**

I awoke early the next day for my first class: Shetland fiddle. I was one of the first people in the class. Everyone dragged in after a late night, complaining of not getting enough sleep. The instructor, Claire White, a Shetland native, was the last person to arrive to class- she had smelled coffee wafting from one of the dining areas and stopped to get some. She was very tall and awake: her jetlag hadn't kicked in yet.

While she took out her fiddle, Claire told us the story behind the first traditional Shetland reel we were to learn: "Faroe Rum-" a tune from the days of cod fishing, when liquor and tobacco were smuggled for home consumption. 'Faroe Rum,' like all the other tunes Claire taught us, was collected by her mentor and fiddle teacher, Dr. Tom Anderson.

After the history of 'Faroe Rum,' Claire taught us the tune the traditional way: by ear. Dr. Tom Anderson was the main proponent in preserving traditional Shetland music. The traditional Shetland fiddling style and the traditional Shetland music in general had all but died out before he started collecting, teaching and performing around the world. His vocation- saving traditional music- is what I hope to achieve in my lifetime. Dr. Anderson, a Shetland native, could understand the dialects of the Shetland Islands, which made it much easer for him to collect traditional music there. To be able to collect music accurately, one must be able to speak the language of that culture.

I am, along with my interest in music, extremely interested in language and linguistics. I am almost fluent in Spanish, and am in my fourth year studying Latin. I hope to eventually learn Breton and Gallego, the languages of Brittany and Galicia, respectively. I hope to immerse myself in languages during college. **(I know I keep saying it, but you gotta admit, this guy Ryan is unique. I'm an educated man and have never heard of Brittany or Galicia, nor their languages of Breton and Gallego)**

There are thousands of endangered languages. Most Native American languages, some Oceanic languages as well as some African languages, just to name a few, are in danger of being lost in the near future. Music, like language, is a form of communication. When a form of ethnic music is lost, it is much the same as if a language is lost: a cultural identity is lost and will never be the same again or will never BE again. **(Interesting analogy)** This is why I want to be an ethnomusicologist: to preserve a vital part of our global heritage, to preserve music that will never be repeated in quite the same way, to preserve the ideas and the processes that are a part of music and its making.

After Shetland fiddling, I headed over to my next class: Icelandic Singing. I took this class last year, and enjoyed it so much that I just had to take it again. I got there and gave the instructor a hug. Bára Grímsdóttir is a teacher from Iceland who is working to revive traditional Icelandic song.

This year, like last year, Bára taught us the rudiments of pronunciation and stylistic details of traditional Icelandic song. She also explained the different forms the traditional music takes in Iceland: drinking songs, ballads, dancing songs, hymns, prayers, gossipy telltale songs, and fables.

While the sun lilted through the beautiful stained glass windows, Bára taught us a song that told the heartbreaking story of a baby killed by its mother who was too poor to keep it. In the song, the baby's ghost offers its poverty-stricken mother its rag so that she may have something to wear to a dance in the next village. I was stunned. Before this past year's Icelandic Singing class, I was familiar with a song in the English singing tradition which tells the story of a nobleman's daughter who gave birth to two babes while she hid in the woods. Because she could not let anyone know she had given birth, she killed them. While she walked back to her father's castle, she met their ghosts. How could cultures so far removed from each other have the same song?

When Bára gave us the background on the song we learned in class, I brought up that there were too many similarities between the songs for it to be a coincidence. This started a class discussion on trans- culturation: stories, songs, melodies and ideas that are found in more than one society. I was ecstatic! Many crimes are the product of a misunderstanding and lack of knowledge between cultures. This proved to me that, if two or more cultures share songs and stories, they were not that different after all.

But why traditional ethnic music and not, say, pop music? Traditional music is composed for many different reasons: to tell a story, to tell of an injustice, to keep an event a part of history and not let it die. It is made to commemorate births, deaths, a coming of age. It is made for community events: dances, funerals.

And pop music? I see pop music as being made for a profit, so that those involved in its production may make money. The music is usually formula-based: a few verses about love and sex with a chorus, which are repeated many times. There is nothing of the depth and tradition that goes into a piece of ethnic music.

(Although it's definitely out of the ordinary, I like the way you're shifting back and forth between the events of the Common Ground events and your own aspirations to mold your future around the music.)

When I came to Icelandic Singing class on Thursday the topics of conversation were not what they had before. Earlier in the week, we had talked with Bára and Bára's husband Chris, a traditional English guitarist, about Icelandic traditions, customs, stories, pronunciation, food and the pieces we were working on. But today it was different. The London Tube Bombings took place today. It was the first I heard about it. Chris is originally from England, though now he lives in Iceland with Bára. After hearing of the bombings, we found out that Chris knew several people who were on the tube when it was bombed, but as far as he knew, they were all safe. After this conversation, we started singing. The piece was an Icelandic hymn, and it never seemed more appropriate.

Everyday, the news tells us of some atrocity that happened in some other part of the world. I never took much notice of them- they happened somewhere else, and were therefore unimportant to my daily routine. I would think "how sad," and move on to the next thought in my mind.

But the London Tube Bombings became very close and personal to me. I have never known anyone involved in a disaster like this before: I knew people who knew someone involved, or I knew someone who knew someone who had died. But I knew Chris very well, and the look on his face- one combining shock and disbelief when we talked about the Tube Bombings- brought the entire disaster into my world.

The incident started me thinking: here I was, sitting in a class, learning the traditional singing style of a culture that I had never thought about, or really even known existed until now. How could I promote musical dialogue between cultures as a way to prevent violence? A quote I remembered from a poster one of my high school teachers had on her wall struck home all of a sudden: "Music may achieve the highest of all missions: she may be a bond between nations, races and states, who are strangers to one another in many ways; she may unite what is disjointed, and bring peace to what is hostile." -Dr. Max Bendiner.

I was already promoting the use of music to prevent violence: I was here at a multi-cultural international gathering, learning from people from different places and cultures with different perspectives. To complete the cycle, I would take what I learned to others and teach them what I was learning. **(Again, I like the smooth transitions between the events of Common Ground and how they affect your thinking about your own future).**

With a college education culminating with a doctorate, I will be able to bring my experiences back to the classroom for my students. As an ethnomusicologist, I will be able to collect, preserve and pass on these traditions to the next generations. I will be able to use the power of music to create dialogues between my students and the cultures they are learning about.

When people learn each other's traditions, they are less likely to be taken in by prejudice and bias and are less likely to resolve their differences with violence. It is true: "Music may achieve the highest of all missions..." It can stop violence, and change the world. My goal, through my education, is to help that change progress: teach the traditions and ideas that surround the music. Complete the cycle before it is broken.

Well done, unique stuff. A very passionate essay from someone who has a very clear vision for his life.

Doesn't hurt that the vision has to do with making the world a better place, either.

Natalie Comer

The greatest show of love for others is through serving them. Love is an action, not merely a feeling. Physical acts of kindness, by way of a smile, a hug, or a laugh as well as through deeds such as giving a cup of water, a bite to eat, or clean clothes are examples of love. Helping others meet their most basic needs from their soul to their physical body are all forms of service.

When I ponder what warms me inside, what fills my heart with love, what challenges me to allow goodness to flow from within me to others, it is when someone has served me. When I have been loved affectionately by someone else, the wellspring of life and love from deep within me pours out to those around me. There is great power in this kind of service. The seeds of trust and regard are planted by acts of love and service. Over time these seeds grow and impact our life in many areas. This type of change is for the good. It is a change that affects a person's well-being as well as the lives in his/her circle of influence. This is my calling: to serve others by loving them so that their outlook on life is more positive, their hope is higher, their love for and trust in others grows, and their life is changed for the good. **(An interesting introduction here. It's rare that you see a person develop a philosophical viewpoint around which they want to shape their lives, and then decide what career path will dovetail with that philosophy. I'm interested to hear more...)**

Over the past two and a half years, I have seen the impact of love and service toward others at the Children's Hospital at the University of Virginia Medical Center. I served as a Patient Care Assistant on 7 Central and 7 West (I assume these are floors in the hospital?). At the hospital, I cared for patients as young as a few days to occasionally 20 year olds. My role in this team of caregivers was to serve and care for the children I was assigned to as well as other children when I was able. While caring for the children, it was imperative that I showed respect to and assisted the families as best I could. Myspecific duties, for each patient in my care, were as follows, but not limited to: measuring vital signs, recording input and output, assisting in activities of daily living, such as: baths, which included oral and hair care; diaper, clothing and linen changes if appropriate and as needed; assisting patients in ambulation, transfers in and out of bed; spending time talking, playing and/or holding patients depending on their age; and always lots of love. **(That last part is a good thing to add; had she admitted the part about "always lots of love," you may have gotten the picture of some growling, uncaring CAN who,** when doing such tasks, is simply going through the motions. We've all encountered people like that in our hospital experiences, I think. It's good to remind grizzled old scholarship judges by myself that there are indeed people who do these sometimes-unpleasant duties with a smile on their faces because they care about people.)

It was at the hospital that my calling was made clearer. In my past, I have always enjoyed working with and being around children. I knew my gift was relating to, caring for, and being with children. I was unsure; however, in what facet this gift would best be invested. Looking back at my past experiences with children, I can now see my life was being steered toward work that focuses on children who are suffering, and in the midst of healing.

Even while attending college in Florida and working part time, clues to my future were being shown to me. I worked at Pediatric Health Choice. This company provided medical supplies and medications to children with special needs. I worked in the office and the pharmacy, and was exposed to the different supplies and medications I would eventually see and use and hear used all around me on the hospital floor. It was here that I remember the first glimpse of my calling. One day I went with a nurse that worked with our company, to a daycare center for special needs children that was fully staffed by nurses. This would be my first real exposure to children with special needs. Seeing a two-year old running around playing while a twenty foot long oxygen tube was attached to him was culture shock to me. At the same time he also deeply touched my heart.

The next pivotal experience happened in Charlotte, NC. I was completing my degree at the University of North Carolina, and wanted to volunteer at the children's hospital in Charlotte. I was only able to volunteer twice due to extenuating circumstances, however, the two visits I had greatly impacted me. The children I met, I have never forgotten. One little girl, about three years old, came into the playroom with her grandmother. The little girl's face appeared very sad as she looked around the room. At one point, I picked up a toy near where she was playing and handed it to her. For some reason, this was so special to her, and her face lit up in a big smile. Her grandmother was so excited. She told me that in the four days since her surgery, this was her first smile. Meetings like these do not happen by coincidence. I was meant to be there. She was meant to touch my life as much as I touched hers. **(I like Natalie's admission that she didn't volunteer at this particular place often before she goes on to tell us how she was affected. Not only is it an honest disclosure, but it** also gives you some insight into her personality to know that she attaches strong meaning -- indeed, believes she was meant to be there - to her experiences at this children's hospital.)

Following this experience, I worked as a nanny and babysat for several different families. One family, with a ten year old boy and twelve year old girl, was in the process of a divorce. Another family lost their mother just two months prior to my meeting them. An eight year old boy and twelve year old girl were trying to cope with such a tremendous loss. The third family included a two year old girl, an eight year old boy and ten year old girl. A few months before I began caring for them, their father had committed suicide. Even though in these families, the children were not ill due to disease, they were still suffering greatly. These experiences readied me in ways I had not imagined for life with ill and injured children. No work or service I have ever done in my life has been more intrinsically rewarding, more satisfying to my soul, and more life changing than working with these special children and their families. **(When she writes this, I believe it, mostly because she's gone into such detail, and with conviction, throughout the essay.)** In a family's greatest time of suffering, to be there to help them in any way, getting them some water, or supplies, or just a listening ear, is an honor. To serve them and be a part of this most delicate time in their lives, is a gift and a blessing to my life. Not only have I been able to be a blessing of love to them, they have done the same for me, and in so doing have forever changed me. The children I have served and loved are a part of me, of my soul, of my history that can never be changed or taken away, and is deeply cherished. **(OK, remember that part of Confessions" where I emphasize that scholarship judges like to give money to people who dedicate themselves to helping other people in some way? Well, you probably won't find a better example than the above paragraph.)**

*John, a nine-year old boy, with leukemia, loved Fruity Pebbles. During a time when it was so hard to get him to eat anything, I brought some in to him, hoping he would eat. He looked up at me with his big brown eyes and said, "Can I give you a hug?"

*Lydia, two years old, with leukemia, came onto the floor riding on her mother's lap in the wheelchair because she couldn't walk at this time. From down the hall she saw me, and called down the floor, in her two year old voice, "Natalie!" just grinning from ear to ear.

*Maria-six years old, cancer-told me that she and her mother prayed for me during their bedtime prayers.

*Lakesha-sixteen years old, post spinal fusion, after helping her walk to the toilet-asked me to wait in the bathroom with her. While we were waiting, she said she wanted to sing me a song, so she proceeded with the most angelic voice to sing to her Father.

*Elizabeth-eight year old girl, cancer-was recovering from major lung surgery where the doctors removed as much cancer as possible. This was a complicated and painful surgery, and for days afterwards Elizabeth was very angry and irritated. She fought us every step of the way when we had to move her or transfer her to the chair to sit up for a while. A few weeks later she came onto the floor, ran up to me, and said, "I love you!" A few months later she was in Heaven.

*Eric-fifteen years old, cancer-was sleeping when I walked in, his mom was reading by the window, we began to talk and she asked for my hands, she began to pray for me, for my hands that touch these special children, my hands that touch families that are hurting, hands that carry water into their rooms, hands that serve and love their children.

(This made me tear up. I wouldn't have the stomach to do what Natalie does. It's a damn good thing there are people like Natalie around, isn't it?)

My hope in becoming a nurse is to continue to serve and impact the lives I touch for good. I hope to work again on the Pediatric floor of UVa's Children's Hospital when my Clinical Nurse Leadership program of education is complete. **(I have no doubt this will happen.)**

Having participated in several seminars and workshops to further my knowledge of the healthcare field, I am thankful that education continues after the completion of a degree.

I also have a deep passion for volunteering in underprivileged areas in the United States and in other countries; to help the poor, widows, and orphans of the world by donating my skills, knowledge, resources, and time to them.

The University of Virginia's School of Nursing's Clinical Nurse Leader (CNL) program seems like the best fit for me, and the direction my path is taking me. I am confident that through the CNL program and the skills I acquire that I will be able to step into the nursing role and succeed. From my experience so far in the health field, I have seen the importance of leaders. In order to maintain a stable and orderly work place, leadership is essential. Confidence in one's role, responsibilities, and quality of work is reflected in the care of the patients and the atmosphere of the workplace. The CNL program seems to be all encompassing and diverse in the types of classes it requires to equip me with the skills I will need to perform at an excellent level as a floor nurse. Being a master's level program, I also feel this program will equip me with a solid foundation to begin a nursing career. As far as my educational goals are concerned, this program would help me attain the knowledge and training required to be an influential member of my future patient's healthcare team. Due to little experience with team management, I am excited about the educational and on the floor training the leadership component of this program will instill in me.

As a leader, there are several characteristics I deem valuable. One's attitude is a huge component in maintaining respectful relationships with his/her co-workers. Being positive, helpful, humble and service minded make up the type of leader I am striving to be. My heart and spirit are aligned in this way **(clearly this is true)** , and I am confident that my time at the UVa School of Nursing will help me acquire the practical skills I need. With the CNL program being a second-degree program, this suits my needs very ell. Having a bachelor's degree in Psychology, I am very thankful to be able to apply this part of my life toward a greater goal. The length of the program also appeals to me being that it will enable me to get out in to the work field relatively soon.

The events, jobs, and experiences I have had in my past have all prepared me for this transition into registered nursing. Every step had to happen, every step was a key to the next door and every step was needed to get me to this very place in my life now. God's timing is perfect. I am excited and look forward to embarking on this journey at the School of Nursing at The University of Virginia.

(I think it'd be hard to find someone who is more committed to her chosen career, and to helping others, as Natalie. Somebody give this girl some scholarship money!)

Cassandra Jones

My name is Casey Jones and I am a professional dancer who stumbled upon this scholarship while searching for a way to pay for the next four years of dental school **(yes, you read that correctly). (Is that a pun, the professional dancer who stumbles onto a scholarship? If so, it's kind of cute.)** With a Physiological Sciences degree in hand from the University of Arizona, I decided to put stability on hold as I opted for an adventure by moving to New York in pursuit of one of my dreams, dancing professionally. There is nothing worse than wondering "what if?" and I never wanted to look back and wish that I had taken the risk. **(Great thought! Looking back and wondering "what if?" is terrible; the only problem is, by the time you're old enough to realize this and integrate it into your life, you're usually much older and already have too many "what ifs?" to look back on! It's a sign of maturity to realize this at a young age, believe me.)** The risk paid off more than I ever imagined when I met my husband on a National Tour of My Fair Lady. After one year of performing apart, we looked to cruise ships as a way to perform together while seeing the world. **(OK, now you're just making me jealous.)** Our lives have been filled with wonderful adventures, but we now crave the stability that we put on hold. Upon the completion of our final ship contract, we moved to Arizona in preparation for my attendance to the Arizona School of Dentistry and Oral Health in July. After our beautiful wedding and a quick honeymoon to New Orleans where we volunteered some of our time to help in the rebuilding efforts following Hurricane Katrina, we began to make our house a "home."

The "upside" of the past six years is that it has been filled with priceless experiences; the "downside" is that we were lacking many of the everyday possessions needed to transition to life on land. The money that we had saved is quickly disappearing as we continue to purchase necessary items such as a bed, car, computer, and various appliances. My first year of tuition alone is $36,570, and although I am looking at this endeavor as an "investment for my future," I also know that every little bit that I can raise in scholarships now will make the inevitable loan repayment process that much easier later. **(True, but wow -- $36,750 is a lot of money for one year of school. Word of advice to everyone out there reading this: When in doubt, choose "cheap" over "prestigious.")** Essentially, the less money I have to borrow the better, and this scholarship would help bring me that much closer to making my next dream become a reality. This scholarship application is only the beginning and I know that you have countless qualified candidates, but if you will indulge me, and "follow my lead," I would like to highlight some of the events in my life that have brought me to a transition from dancer to doctor.

I wish I could say I wanted to be a dentist since I was young. Progressing in a linear fashion to achieve that goal would have been more practical and straightforward, but far less diversified and enlightening than my more complicated route. (Judges understand this. Linear progression in life is very rare indeed.) Instead of a straight progression from undergraduate work to dental school, my path can be likened to a "dance" of sorts, with many turns and a few "leaps of faith." This freestyle footwork has helped me acquire additional skills and personal insights that have brought me to this point in my journey. **(The dance metaphor works well here, I think. Carry on...)**

Two such distinctly different interests paved divergent paths that, until now, left me feeling torn and obligated to choose just one. My love of dance led me into college as a Dance major, but my love of science prompted me to change that major to Physiological Sciences. I became involved in sleep apnea research that resulted in my first publication. The hands-on experience and satisfaction of performing meticulous surgical procedures on the upper airways of laboratory rats in preparation for data collection was of particular interest to me.

Upon graduating from college, I left my science path to follow a completely different path. In a "leap of faith," I packed up my Honda and drove all the way from my home in Arizona to New York in pursuit of one of my dreams. Before landing a role in "West Side Story," a national tour of "My Fair Lady," and various other productions that took me to Amsterdam, Australia, London, Paris, Mexico, and Tokyo, I scraped by for a year on "survival jobs." To survive in New York as a professional dancer, talent needs to be accompanied by a strong business sense. A performer's entire career is essentially a series of countless interviews ("auditions"), extensive networking, and flexible scheduling.

The combination of a dance career augmented by "survival jobs" has made me an excellent communicator and has honed my time management and "real life" business skills. **(Casey uses "quotation marks" around phrases "too often" for "no reason," but I'm willing to forgive it here because she's got an otherwise great essay going here.)**

The need to supplement my performance career with "survival jobs," allowed me to sample many other career possibilities. Such an eclectic past has only made me more certain of my next step. Each experience ranging from dance teacher to legal secretary and from executive assistant to babysitter has enriched my life and added to my palate of interests and experience. By obtaining my ACE Personal Trainer Certification and becoming involved in fitness videos with Denise Austin and David Kirsch, I was able to incorporate science into a survival job. Through carefully prepared fitness programs based on individualized needs, desires, and goals, as a personal trainer I successfully improved each client's self-image by creating stronger, healthier bodies. I thoroughly enjoyed providing inspiration and motivation for everyone that I worked with, but I craved more science.

The professor who sponsored my sleep apnea research in college connected me with the Sleep Disorders Center of the Department of Medicine at New York University, which led to my second publication. I enjoyed the systematic discipline supporting the sleep study research, but with the majority of my time spent performing computer analysis, I missed the hands-on experience of my college research. I also needed a break from the outrageous New York rents, so when I was offered a chance to perform on a cruise ship, I jumped at the opportunity to travel the world, reflect on my two loves, and plan my future.

My earliest exposure to dentistry was through my orthodontist and pediatric dentist. My orthodontist made such a difference in my smile that I still talk about my drastic before and after pictures whenever someone compliments my smile. I affectionately refer to the "before" picture as my "prehistoric animal teeth," and continue to marvel at the way the enormous gap between my two front teeth literally closed before my eyes in the first day of having braces. My toothy metal grin even graced the television screen as I competed in the dance category of Ed McMahon's "Star Search '90."

I felt so comfortable with my pediatric dentist that I continued to go to him until I graduated from high school. On my last visit, he gave me an additional "graduation" ceremony where he took my picture with a certificate for the "Dental Dean's List" (my "diploma"), and handed me a referral to an "adult" dentist. These fond memories along with my love of children tell me that I want to consider going beyond general dentistry to specialize in orthodontics or pediatric dentistry.

My most recent desire to pursue dentistry resulted from my mother, who has been going through extensive reconstruction of her misaligned bite. I started exploring the possibility and observed several dentists in action. I am convinced I have found a way to build a bridge between the two roads of my life. My extensive exploration of possible careers has revealed a way for me to blend art and science in dentistry. I love bringing smiles to people's faces, and have devoted the last four years doing that through entertainment. Now, I have the unique opportunity to use my artistic ability to literally create and polish those smiles.

The more I discover about dentistry, the more I believe that it should be my life's work. Regardless of the twists and turns that this path may bring, I am convinced the choreography of my life has led me to a profession that will allow me to combine my diverse interests to provide "my audience" with the best from both of my two loves. To quote a well-known musical, "A Chorus Line," I now have the ever-present urge to belt at the top of my lungs, "I can do that . . . That I can do!" Now, as I complete this essay, I can only hope that you are still reading and that you will consider "casting me" for this scholarship because I can assure you that my "performance" will not disappoint.

(A clever use of the dancing metaphor in the closing, bringing it all full circle. Overall, it's a great essay that shows Casey's dedication to helping people through dentistry, and also shows by her past accomplishments that she'll be a great investment of scholarship money regardless of what she decides to do. From the sound of her essay, it won't be long before she's starting the League of Dancing Dentists. Would it surprise you? Not me.)

TJ Warschefsky

3, 2, 1...Liftoff! The earth shook, the sky illuminated, and everybody stood in awe. My Uncle Jerry had just blasted into outer space for a five month stay aboard the space station MIR. Noticing the tears running down everyone's face, it was right then that I told myself I, too, would accomplish something significant one day. I wanted to have an impact on people, and I wanted to make a difference. I would learn in the following years that making a difference comes in many forms and finding my niche would be my challenge. **(Nice intro... it's unique that he was actually present as his uncle was blasted into space, and I can see how the reaction of the crowd might be one of those moments that inspired you to do great things of your own. I'm intrigued...)**

In my Uncle's book, he wrote: "Specialization is for insects. Man should be able to change a diaper, run a marathon, build a house, write a book, appreciate good music, and fly in space." I value a balanced lifestyle and think it is important to be well-rounded in order to interact with people of varying backgrounds and beliefs **(A mature thought from a young adult. Nice to hear).** I knew I would someday have to modify the last part of my uncle's quote about flying in space, and replace it with whatever I found my passion to be.

I always wanted a career where I would wake up every morning and be excited to go to work. **(Don't we all!)** Perhaps that is why it took me such a long time to decide on a career. There were many tasks that I was skilled in, and there were aspects of certain jobs that I enjoyed, but I always knew there was that perfect niche waiting for me. There are three principal responsibilities that I desire for my profession; I want to be a businessman, I want to be a doctor, and I want to be community leader and family-man.

I began a lawn business when I was in seventh grade, and business has always come naturally to me. My entrepreneurial spirit and talent in business drew me to Albion College, where I would study liberal arts and major in business. At Albion College, I planned to compete on the tennis and cross country teams, and I received scholarships in both the Gerstacker Honors Institute for Professional Management and the Ford Institute for Public Policy and Service. The public policy program appealed to me because it allowed me to continue my community service. I got involved in many campus organizations, including being

Treasurer of the Investment Club, the Vice-President of the Albion College Pre-Dental Club, and a member of the national service fraternity, Alpha Psi Omega. **(Note: this is a service fraternity and therefore isn't what I refer to in the section on Greek life)**

During my very first semester, I left campus to help out with an urgent illness in my family. My professors allowed me to complete my courses, although some professors chose to give me "credit" instead of a letter grade. I was told that it would reflect poorly on my transcript, but I was willing to accept that consequence to help my family.

I returned that spring with more direction and a change of heart. I knew I wanted to be in health-care, because I wanted to help others. I realize that is a stereotypical response, however, it strikes a much more personal note for me. My step-father suffers from multiple sclerosis, and I have taken on the responsibility of "man of the house" and "caregiver" for as long as I can remember **(YES! Remember what I said about telling the committee about your responsibilities within your own family? This is a perfect example)**. Helping him and my family always gave me so much satisfaction. As a doctor, a dentist is prepared to work with their hands every day and yield noticeable results; while at the same time diagnosing a multitude of other health-related measures. I knew that I had to find something that allowed me to interact with and help people, and my extensive business skills and creativity could be utilized in running my own office. I was determined to complete my studies in business and public policy, but I also began courses for a pre-health career path **(A mature choice, blending science with business. If he follows through, TJ will be very well-off someday.)**

Organization, time management, discipline, and an exceptional memory had always been strong aspects of my character **(Ditto, then, what I just said about probably making it big someday).** However my intense course-load **(including online and summer courses)**, community service **(both at home and at college)**, varsity sports, work, and extra-curricular involvement were an obvious over-commitment. I was able to manage my numerous obligations and activities, but realized that I needed to narrow my pursuits in order to be most effective and efficient. I gained valuable insight from this period of over-commitment, as it taught me how to handle the boundaries of my limits and the importance of a balanced lifestyle. **(Mature observation. In most cases, students recount this load of activities with a trite phrase like "I stay busy managing my friends, work, lass, etc.," but TJ gleans the lesson that too much is too**

much. As you can tell, TJ is painting a picture of himself as a pretty mature guy, which is the advice I give in "Confessions")

My internship experience with a CPA and financial planning firm verified that I would not enjoy a desk job. I needed to be on my feet and interacting with people. I sought out the career development office and took career interest and personal inventories. My love for volunteerism, outstanding eye-hand coordination, interest in art and piano, work ethic, people skills, drive and motivation for success, knack for business, and my leadership traits—all combined to reveal that dentistry was the profession for me **(Wow, I'd have never put that together. But come to think of it, I guess that stuff would all make you a good dentist).** I felt as though I could have a more significant and successful impact on the lives of others if I translated those business skills and applied them to a greater cause. As a dentist, business skills are particularly important, as each patient I will treat is essentially a client; but at the same time I am able to further their health and well-being.

I contacted every dentist I knew and began to observe at every opportunity. I even found a dental office where I could observe on a Saturday. I shadowed Oral Surgeons, Endodontists, Implant Specialists, and Orthodontists. From my very first observation, I knew that I was going to be a dentist. I loved interacting with patients, and was interested in the concerns and strategies for oral health care and disease prevention. My love of school and learning is a perfect match, and I truly could not wait to begin my studies and career as a dentist.

It is becoming increasingly apparent that dentists are often the very first health care practitioners to recognize and diagnose medical problems. These ailments include diabetes, obesity, cardiovascular disease, cancer, eating disorders, and ADHD, among many others. **(Fascinating. I had no idea this was the case. And if a judge is, at any point, fascinated by your essay, that's a good thing.)** After just one semester in dental school, I have been amazed at the significant impact a dentist can have on the overall health and well-being of their patients. Dentists are not typically thought of as "doctors" in the wider health spectrum of the word, although numerous lives are saved each and every day because of a head, neck, and oral cavity examination performed by dentists and their resulting referrals.

In addition to recognition and diagnosis of several illnesses, the more specific oral-health care that dentists provide to their patients has a significant impact on their overall quality of life. Research has shown that oral health influences emotional, as well as physical, characteristics of every day lives.

Individuals with poor oral health often miss work or school due to pain. Also, the increasing emphasis on cosmetic dentistry proves that it frequently results in a lack of self-confidence and embarrassment. Studies on children have revealed that one of the most common types of criticism they receive is related to their teeth, which can have a considerable impact on their emotional development **(He's right. I'm a lot older than TJ, and I remember kids getting teased because of their teeth all the time).**

With the baby boomer population advancing into the category of senior citizenship, the focus on this age group is becoming much more relevant. Lack of self-confidence and poor-nutrition are two of the major categories that result in the poor health of the elderly. Technology in dentistry has made it possible to treat patients of all ages and conditions, and can surely assist the elderly in their quality of life.

As a dentist, I am undertaking one of the most diversified occupations in terms of the responsibilities I have and the impact that can result. I am immensely intrigued with the opportunity to not only help the population have healthier and stronger teeth, but to also recognize other life-threatening diseases, help with the emotional security that comes with cosmetics, and relieve the stresses and pains that can so profoundly arise from poor oral-health. My uncle lived up to the cliché of reaching for the stars. (Way to come full circle!) While I may not be flying among the stars, I have found the perfect goal for me. To modify his quote: "Specialization is for insects. Man should be able to change a diaper, run a marathon, build a house, write a book, appreciate good music, and fill a cavity."

A mature and interesting essay from a kid who has tons of promise, and those are the kind of kids we like to give scholarships to. Very well done.

Cheryl Rhodes

Throughout my childhood, I was blessed with the ignorance of assuming life was a day in the park and the world was my playground. I was born the third child of four to two loving parents: a nurturing stay-at-home mother whose days revolved around her children's needs, and a well-respected physician father who successfully owned a family practice that generously provided my family with what most would consider an enviable life. We lived in the biggest house on the block. It consisted of a huge backyard swimming pool, diving board and slide, hot tub, a two-story tree house, and a deck area that proved perfect for neighborhood parties, family reunions and the like. We drove nice cars, and my siblings and I attended an expensive private school, enowned for its incredible student teacher ratio, encouraging environment, and hands-on learning approach. My family went on annual summer vacations to places like Disney World, Grand Canyon, and Yellowstone National Park, to mention a few. This is what I considered "normal" living, as I had not known anything different since my birth.**(Great introduction here -- paints a great picture of her young life while setting us up for a blow of bad news. It's also mechanically perfect.)**

My sense of reality suffered a huge blow when, at the age of ten, I came home from school one day and turned on the television. Given no previous warning, I watched the day's top news story in complete shock and horror as I stared at my father's mug shot. I watched reports of his drug addiction, his theft of prescription medications at a local doctor's office, and his resulting arrest. In the coming months, my family's reputation would switch from one of admiration to one of empathy and gossip. My friends and their parents knew, my teachers and school administrators knew, my coaches knew, and people whom I had never met before in my life all knew about the struggles that my family and I endured while my dad was in a constant battle to fight and overcome his drug addiction. **(Yep, there's the blow I was expecting. Well-written.)**

As soon as my family escaped the downfalls of the media spotlight, we were forcefully thrown right back into it's calamity when my oldest brother, Greg, was hit by a car driving well over 60 mph, killing him instantly. He was 18 years old. I would never talk, play, or fight with Greg again...his absence hurt far worse than any rumor, gossip, or speculation ever could. Needless to say, previous problems were now seemingly benign.

Greg's untimely death was extremely hard on everyone, and it did nothing but fuel my father's addiction. My parents were constantly fighting with one another, and in an attempt to save their marriage, they decided to separate. My brother Stephan became increasingly withdrawn, and my sister, Melanie, and I were essentially numbed by the whole situation, spurred by the overwhelming sorrow and confusion that constantly surrounded us.

Despite several stints in rehab and multiple attempts at recovery, my father lost his long and arduous battle with addiction. He overdosed on prescription drugs and was found dead in his apartment at around three o'clock on a Monday morning. This was devastating, and quite frankly, nearly unbearable. As young as I was, his funeral brought me no sense of closure. Rather, seeing his lifeless body and touching his cold, folded hands only increased my overwhelming feelings of sadness, fear, and loss.

(Wow... this is a devastating set of paragraphs. In a couple of pages, Cheryl has taken us from a perfect childhood to absolute hell. You can't set the scene much better than this.)

By the age of fifteen, I had lived nearly seven years in the unhealthy environment of a drug addict; one that was filled with innumerable lies, countless broken promises, and an unending concern for my own safety and well-being as well as that of my father's. I lost my brother Greg, whom growing up I secretly idolized and emulated, to the cruel uncertainties of life and I lost my father, my endlessly caring dad who I loved more than any words can possibly convey, to a long and tumultuous drug addiction. To make matters worse, my family received stares in public, we were victim to rumor and hearsay, and we were sought by hounding reporters who had the audacity to approach our home in hopes of covering the next big cover story. Reality check: Life is not easy, it is not fair, and it is not guaranteed. **(A mature observation, although no surprise given what she went through during this time.)**

I was forced to deal with some of life's harshest truths at a very young age. While they remain as the most trying times in my life and have been tremendous challenges to my emotional, physical, and mental stability, these setbacks have undoubtedly made huge contributions to person that I am today: a strong, independent, hard-working and goal-oriented woman who refuses to fall at the face of adversity. **(Remember what I said in "Confessions" about talking about adversity and then showing how you've bounced back from it and began to turn things around? This is exactly what I mean.)**

I graduated high school in May of 2003 and attended the University of North Texas the following fall. My freshman year I maintained a 4.0 grade point average and have since sustained high academic achievement. The university's central housing system has employed me as a Resident Assistant, a job that assists students from various walks of life in their transition from high school to college. The job also serves as an outlet for students needing advice, support, and encouragement. I have taken initiative in donating my time to the community by participating in various charitable opportunities. This past April I took part in a fundraising vent, the Denton Relay for Life, a twelve hour walk benefiting the American Cancer Society. Serving as my team's captain, I proudly led in our collaborative success of raising well over $1300 for the cause. I received true personal reward while helping in the relief efforts for hurricanes Katrina and Rita. I was fortunate to have the opportunity to volunteer my time and participate in various games, group activities and individual reading sessions with dozens of children displaced by the hurricanes. College has provided me with experiences both inside the classroom and out, that render me forever grateful.

Completion of a postsecondary program is extremely important to me because it is the first of many steps in bringing me closer to my goals. I have an unexplainable love for every aspect of television and film production and look forward to finding work in the field upon graduation. I would first, however, like to attend graduate school and work towards receiving a Master's degree, enabling me to eventually pursue work as a college professor. The thought of teaching students and instilling the knowledge that I've gained through my postsecondary education as well as my personal experiences brings promising feelings of accomplishment and satisfaction. I would find it very rewarding to influence students who love this field of study in a positive way.

Though I look forward to a future career in teaching, I am also adamant that I test the waters of the industry for myself. My determination is strong but my passion is even stronger. Imagining that I can write my thoughts, experiences, and beliefs into a script, visually capture those images on film, and use the art of editing to formulate those mere initial thoughts into a cohesive story absolutely fascinates me. While I am aware that the expression of personal convictions opens wide doors to opposition and criticism, knowing that there is a slight chance of even one person being positively impacted is liberating.

I also understand that the entertainment industry is regarded as ruthless and viciously competitive. Strange as this may seem, I consider this a perk. I want mistakes, I want hurdles, and I want an occasional road block that forces me to take the detoured route. These challenges and inconveniences are the very instances that provide us with the opportunities to prevail. These challenges force us to focus in on where we are in our lives and how far we have come. But most importantly, in overcoming these challenges we reinforce the affirmations that surviving the bumpy road, though sometimes hard and unyielding, is far more rewarding than the indolent road of monotony. Mediocrity is something that I refuse to settle for. In everything that I do, I strive for excellence. **(Excellence, not perfection. Excellence is great.)**

Personal goals and expectations that I have set, and continue to set for myself are the backbone of who I am and they certainly influence everything that I do. As cliché as it may sound, I am grateful for everything that I have experienced in my past, both the good and the bad, because learning from those experiences is what continues to provide me with the initiative to overcome any odds put forth against me. **(When you're talking about the sort of things that you went through as a child, that definitely does NOT sound like a cliche.)** Where many would give up, I have pulled through and thrived to become a very driven woman whose dedication and hard-work have ultimately paid big dividends. Completion of a postsecondary program is something I look forward to as it will unquestionably bring me another step closer to pursuing work in an industry I love, and one day becoming college professor. In wrapping up the final semesters of my college education, I know that my post-graduate future will be benefited by the many lessons I've learned towards reaching success, but I have no intentions of stopping there, for continued learning and personal growth are life's biggest dividends of all.

(An essay that's exemplary of a concept I often in mention in "Confessions" -- that of enduring obstacles, overcoming them, and using them to fuel your own comeback. Congrats to Cheryl on a great essay, not to mention all the achievements that made it possible!)

Bonnie Jones

I stood in front of an adorable two story cottage with a white picket fence around the yard and flower beds in their full glory. The home radiated the image of small town America. I grabbed several bags of intricately sewn teddy bears and threw them over my shoulder as if I were Santa. I took a deep breath and marched out of the public eye and into a world that I didn't know existed, much less understood. Inside the walls were children running, mothers talking, and women filling out paperwork; inside the storybook cottage was a haven, a shelter for abused women and children. Word spread rapidly that I was there to give presents, and the children flocked around more quickly than I could open the bags of teddy bears. One child immediately fell in love, and she snuck off to a corner hugging her new friend and chattering away as if the bear would surely carry on an elaborate conversation with her. Another child struggled to decide on which bear would be hers. She traded a dozen times before deciding on a bear that was red with a plaid tummy and ears. However, the child that I remember most clearly was a little boy about four or five years old. He grabbed up his teddy bear, sternly proceeded to a corner, and began crying and pummeling the bear. I stood there with crocodile tears in my eyes, unsure of what to do, and feeling very much like a failure. **(Wow. That is a powerful opening paragraph. Especially the end, of course.)**

After that experience, I slowly faded away from working with children. I spent less time working in nurseries and working with the Daisy Girl Scout troop that I had led. I spent more time with elders for awhile, and finally, ended up working with architects. Surely, this would be easier than seeing a child emotionally reenact a behavior that he learned somewhere. Despite my pink shirts and high heels, most of the rather gruff men I worked with grew to respect my design talents, and I proceeded to actively pursue scholarships to architecture and design schools in North Carolina and South Carolina.

My love for children and their wellbeing did not fade though, and I grew very dissatisfied with spending hours interacting with none other than my computer. I missed their smiles; I missed them reaching up to hold my hand with their pudgy little hands, but mostly I missed watching them grow. Childhood is a time that rapidly shapes who we will become, and I missed watching the discovery and enthusiasm a child experiences. **(So far, this is great storytelling. I can't put a finger on why, honestly --it just is.)**

About the time that Clemson University informed me of my scholarship to study architecture, a precious gift came into my life, David. David is my godson; his mother, Holly, is my best friend. I knew Cleveland County had one of the highest teen pregnancy rates in the state. I had talked with many of my friends when they were uncertain of how to talk to their families about their pregnancies, but it never really hit me until it was Holly. The pregnancy was the beginning of many difficult times to come. Her boyfriend became an aggressive alcoholic. After David was born, he disappeared. All of the sudden because of my love for Holly, I had to face children again. How could I do it? I knew that one day we would have to tell this precious child why his daddy was not around. I knew that it was going to be hard with Holly and me both working and in school, but as I set there holding David on October 17, 2002, I didn't care. All I knew is that I had never been so deeply in love.

The year continued as I wrestled with what I should do with my life. Clemson was the closest school to David, so I decided I would attend the university and figure out my life later. (This is an impressive commitment. I can't recall hearing of anyone go to such lengths for one's godson.) However, a trip to Europe confirmed my path early because I saw my natural gravitation towards children in some of the

underprivileged areas that I stayed. I returned from Europe, and announced to my family that I was no longer interested in a career in architecture. They were shocked, but incredibly supportive.

When I reached Clemson, I quickly found my path as a Public Health Science major. My family laughed as they recalled the curly headed child who when asked if she too was going to work in the health field would firmly reply, "I'm smarter than that." I had seen the struggles of my mother, a development child psychologist, when she was faced with impossible situations. I had talked through many problems with my father, grandfather, aunt and uncle who were all medical doctors. In my mind, I knew better than to face people who were set in their ways, litigations and endless piles of paperwork, but sociology got the best of me. I knew that this was my purpose in life.

Research and policy quickly became interests of mine at Clemson, so I took an internship at Radiant Research and Greer OBGYN. The internship helped me realize the importance of coordinating the health of children with the health of their parents. The internship was specifically for writing a clinical drug trial to modify a drug called Depo-Provera because in some populations it causes drastic bone loss, even osteoporosis, in very young women. However, much of my time was spent working in an OBGYN clinic with women. My heart raced as I watched babies in three dimensional ultrasound pictures. I deeply enjoyed talking to mothers about breast feeding and nap times for their baby. It was in this internship that I truly affirmed my destiny to work with children, but I also learned that I loved research, policy and working with parents.

A spark was lit after my experience with the children from Greer OBGYN. I signed up to work with the International Foundation for the Medical Relief of Children. We raised money and collected items to be sent to children all over the world. Recently, I was offered the honor of traveling to Costa Rica to work with children on their nutrition and wellness. As I anxiously wait for December, I wonder not only if I will help these children, but I also wonder what they will have to teach me. (By this point, the committee is well aware that Bonnie is not just someone who likes kids and has taken a job doing what she likes; it's obvious that she'll be pouring herself into the well-being of children around her with the same vigor she would've brought to architecture or any other field.)

My internship at Radiant Research also directed me to another internship site that I will work at during the spring of 2006. I was offered a position with the Child Life program at Greenville Hospital System. Here I will spend time with children who are dealing with the stress of illnesses and hospitals. We'll spend time using 'medical play' to explain surgeries, intravenous punctures, and other procedures. I'll also spend time listening to them and trying to find ways to help them not only deal with their environment, but enjoy it while they are there.

There are other various experiences and attributes, both positive and negative, which will help me in future social work settings. One of my true weaknesses is the desire to make every circumstance better and positive for everyone involved, and while college has shown me that this is impossible, I still desire to keep a positive attitude about situations. **(Taking a page from my upcoming resume book, Bonnie knows that if you're ever going to talk about a weakness, it's best to talk about a weakness that is actually a strength. It's true that Bonnie can't make things better for everyone she meets, but are we really going to hold this against her and call it a "weakness"? Of course not.)** Though I do have this weakness of overly caring, I have become more aware of it and find that being aware of is actually one of my strengths. I have learned to step back and assess situations frequently. This way I take care of myself; thus, I can continue to care for others. In speaking with a friend that is a social worker, she also told me that one of the hardest parts to her job is being comfortable in intimidating situations or environments. I know that as a petite female I am at a disadvantage in many environments. However, my training in martial arts will make it easier for me to go into some settings than it would be for most students. Contrary to what most people think, martial arts train you to learn how not to fight.

I believe another asset that I have is my experience with research grants, policies, protocols, diplomacy, and coordination. It is often said, "no margin, no mission," and I have spent significant amounts of time lobbying for money to support programs such as my thesis and the clinical drug trial that I wrote. I have become certified by the National Coalition Building Institute in diversity issues. I also have been certified by both the NIH and CITI to complete research with human subjects. Jobs teaching and tutoring have helped me learn how to communicate with people better, and I have extensive training in various models of behavior change.

At the conclusion of my experience at Clemson University, I hope to continue building my skills at University of North Carolina at Chapel Hill. As I spent hours looking for the perfect graduate program, I discovered the double masters program in Social Work and the Science of Public Health with an emphasis in maternal and child health. I couldn't have designed a program more suited for my dreams. After this, I hope to continue my education by earning my M.D. to become a pediatric oncologist. It is my goal, my dream, to work with children who need to cry and pulverize teddy bears. If I had the proper skill set, I now see that the time in the shelter could have been an opportunity for growth rather than disappointment. Next time, I would like to be able to approach that child and know how to help and how to break that cycle of abuse.

Childhood is such an impressionable time. I was blessed with a supportive and loving family, but not everyone is as blessed as I. In the words of Hemingway, all I ask is for the opportunity to help these children become, "strong in the broken place."

(In sports, when fans are rating the performance of the officials, it's often said that the referees are at their best when you notice them the least. A similar maxim holds here: often the best essays are the ones that inspire the least commentary from me! Clearly, Bonnie is incredibly committed to her life and career with children, and would be deserving of any scholarship money that comes her way. What more can I say?)

Alison Stinely

My first piece is sealed tightly in a family photo album. It is about three by four inches in dimension: I enjoyed working on smaller surfaces then. I believe the medium was a blue Bic ballpoint pen; I had not yet discovered anything beyond crayons and washable markers. I was two years old and not able to write my own name. My mother signed and dated the piece for me. It was a smiley face, which was a bit trite, but hey, it made it into the family photo album anyway. **(Clever intro with an easy style. I like it.)**

It is strange my parents never saved the piece of paper on which I printed my name for the first time but they saved my first piece of artwork. There must be something special about this art stuff.

Soon after the creation of Smiley Face, I graduated to a more sophisticated medium: finger paint. I even dabbled with three dimensional forms, as well. Sure, my parents supplied me with plenty of Barbie Dolls, doll houses and all of the other fancies little girls enjoy. I loved playing with all of those toys, but nothing compared to tinkering with my paint and building blocks. Nothing was greater than creating at my small work table, or crouching on the floor, constructing with those primary colored, three- dimensional shapes.

Although I was not aware of it at the time, I was particularly obsessed with visual balance. I became upset if I were trying to build a doorway with my building blocks and did not have the correct piece to mirror the one on the opposite side. I would have to find smaller blocks to put together to balance the shape on the other side. It makes sense to me now, 18 years later, but I suppose I was a tad obsessive for a three year old.

As I grew, so did my love for the visual arts. Many cousins and a few uncles on both sides of my family, as well as some close family friends, were all excellent artists. A great uncle was an illustrator for Macmillan Publishing Company, who went on to become the art director of Colonial Williamsburg. I grew up surrounded by the visual arts my whole life.

There was one person, in particular, whom I admired most. You will not find his work in textbooks or even at the corner gallery, but he is superbly talented and a visual genius. That man is my father, Patrick Stinely. When I was very young, I can remember rummaging through his portfolios of artwork. I remember being amazed as I watched him work on his latest piece. I would say to myself, "I want to be able to do that." **(And reading this makes a father think, "I want my daughter to think the same thing about me!)**

My art education as a child was limited to my father's instruction. He taught me the use of color, line and light, and how to draw from life by measuring and checking angles. Cutting and pasting in the art room of a grade school does not teach the basic principles and elements of art. My father took the time to introduce me to new techniques and media. The use of shellac or graphite powder to tone paper or turpentine to melt graphite, are techniques many do not learn until later in life. Thanks to my father, I was utilizing them at a young age. **(What a great gift from your father... clearly his effect on you was deep and abiding to this day!)**

As I matured, I realized art was a major part of my life. I made the decision to attend Villa Maria Academy because of the stellar art program it offered. The art scholarship I received my freshman year directed me toward visual arts, my primary focus in high school. Following the obligatory Intro. to Art course, I went on to enroll in every art course Villa offered. These included photography, ceramics, drawing, painting, commercial design and art history. After completing every art course my high school offered, I devoted independent time in the Villa Art Studio to concentrate further on selected media, and to fulfill specific credit hours.

I was active in many extracurricular activities that focused on the arts. I was a member of the National Art Honor Society for three consecutive years. I devoted many hours of service to The Neighborhood Art House, a local charity for underprivileged children. **(A great example of letting the judges know that not only do you enjoy your passions for your own sake, but you also use them as a way to help the community. Committees love this.)** I assisted the children while they participated in visual and performing arts activities after school. I took part in Villa Maria's 24 hour Art-a-Thon where students raised money for a local art charity through sponsorship. We drank absurd amounts of coffee and stayed up all day and night working on the art project of our choice.

Every year I entered pieces in Villa's Spring Show. During my junior year I served as chairperson for the event. Many of the pieces I submitted received first place ribbons, and one piece, entered during my senior year, won the "Best of Show" ribbon. This piece advanced to the Congressional Art Competition in Edinboro, Pennsylvania, where it received an "Honorable Mention" award.

I continued to be recognized during my senior year. I won a calendar cover design for the adjacent township of Millcreek. The calendar was sent to every home in the Millcreek Township area. I won a cash award for placing first in an anti-tobacco poster design contest sponsored by a local non-profit group. I also won the Villa "Senior Art Award," and my name is now engraved on a plaque that will forever hang in my alma mater. Two of my works were featured in the Erie Times-News, in an article about local, upcoming art exhibits.

I participated in the Advanced Placement Portfolio Program, earning three college credits. I also took part in Villa's Senior Project Program, a year-long, optional activity for Villa Seniors. Students must plan an event, research a topic or develop an alternate project. They must choose a teacher who will mentor them through the process and they must document all aspects of the project through dated journal entries that will, subsequently, be signed by their mentor. At the end of the school year, they must assemble a binder of all important documents and photos pertaining to their project, put together a PowerPoint presentation of the same and write a final essay about the entire process.

As part of my project, I decided to use the portfolio that I created through the AP guidelines, along with other works created through my high school career, to hold a one- day exhibit of my work at a local private club. After months of painting, drawing, writing and event planning, the show went off without a hitch. I sold my first piece of artwork to a man who was eating lunch in the club that day and happened to wander into the private room filled with friends, family and faculty. It was a strenuous process, to say the least, but I received the highest ranking from the Senior Project Board, Outstanding with Distinction, making all the stress worthwhile.

During my graduation ceremony I was awarded the Meade Art Scholarship, a cash award given to one graduate seeking an education in the arts. I used the scholarship to buy art supplies, many of which have been used to create the works in my portfolio.

I have spent the past few years building my portfolio, participating in community art events, selling as many pieces as possible and working as a waitress/bartender in between. I helped to organize, and participated in, a fine-art auction at a local upscale restaurant. The money generated from ticket sales was given to a local charity, and the event helped me sell two of my works. During the auction, I was

approached by the Editor in Chief of Art-E-Fakt magazine, who offered me a cover story in the publication. **(Clearly Alison is passionate about art and destined to be an artist forever. Her essay convinces me of this.)**

I have also been a sponsored "Chalk Walk" artist in Erie's own Celebrate Erie festival for two years in a row. The "Chalk Walk" is five blocks of Erie's main street where businesses commission artists to create 10x15 feet murals of any artwork. During the first year, I was asked to recreate Dali's Timepieces. For the second year, I executed an advertisement, of my own design for a local restaurant.

Nowadays, in between fetching dinner orders and mixing drinks, I ruminate about where I want to be and what I want to do, and I have finally figured it out. There is something special about this art stuff, I have known it since the age of two, and I want to be a part of it for the rest of my days. Inasmuch as I have tried to remain involved with art while working at a variety of jobs, I know that the lifestyle I am seeking can only be attained through a higher education. I would like to acquire that education at the Cleveland Institute of Art.

I could read Drawing on the Right Side of the Brain a thousand times over, and memorize it word for word or I could spend months walking through The Louvre studying masterworks, but nothing would compare to the knowledge, skill and insight that I would receive from an excellent education at the Cleveland Institute of Art.

Subjectivity and personal opinions will always be realities of the visual art world. No matter how wonderful some people may think my work is, there will always be some who will disagree, and there is nothing wrong with that **(a humble and mature observation).** That is what it's about,

"Art for Art's Sake." No one artist will ever know everything there is to know about art, and no one artist will ever work in every artistic medium or discipline, but I think one should try. I want to be one who tries. I aspire to understand and experience all that I can and I know that the Cleveland Institute of Art can offer that to me. I also know that in today's world, being an excellent and talented artist is not all that it takes. A degree (or two) and proper education is required if one wishes to survive in today's job market.

I still look through my father's portfolios of work and admire his talent. It upsets me that he did not use his extraordinary abilities to get him where he should be today. He didn't take the proper steps and now owns a business that requires him to perform back-breaking work, six days a week, to help take care of his responsibilities.

I want to take the proper steps to be where I should be in years to come. I am willing to work as hard as I have to in order to get there. From a smiley face portrait done in blue ink, to my most recent self portrait done in oil, art is my life and there is always room to learn and grow. I hope that I will be able to do both at the Cleveland Institute of Art.

I hope she does, too -- she's got a great vision for her life and has been preparing herself for it ever since she was a little girl. Well done!

Caecilia Wyman

In the fall of 1984 I met Mrs. Maslowski, my first grade teacher. She was like a magician, always having the answers to my endless questions. Her patience, energy, and enthusiasm never wore down, and she awoke in me a desire to learn. Inspired by Mrs. Maslowski I had found my destination: I was going to become a teacher. Over the years, the names and faces of people influencing my path have changed. Teachers, family members and countries that I visited, as well as learning another language, helped me become the person that I am now. However, at the age of twenty-seven I have to confess that I have NOT reached my goal. It seems that life had little detours in store for me. Nevertheless, I rose to all challenges and still keep pursuing my dream. Some time ago I stumbled upon a Chinese proverb that kept me focused throughout hard times. It says: "Don't be afraid to move slow, but be afraid of standing still". I may have moved very slowly, but I refuse to stand still and am convinced that I will eventually reach my goal. When I look upon my past I see that the various people and countries that influenced my life come together as a unit-- Me. I know that pieces from my past, combined with future ones will help me to become a unique, dedicated, and fun teacher.

(This is an interesting approach -- telling us that she's always wanted to be teacher, but admitting that it's taken longer than she ever expected. Now that she's reassured me, as a judge, that she's undeterred, I'm interested in hearing more about these challenges.)

Support, strength, optimism, and resilience were life's first important lessons given to me by my family and home, a small town on the communist side of Germany. My parents raised us in a Lutheran household, despite the fact that the East German regime did not approve of religion. My mother was not allowed to be a teacher, since she would not give up her religious beliefs. On November 9th, 1989, people tore down the Berlin Wall and ended the totalitarianism of the communist regime. Everything changed! People did not know what to expect. Uncertainty and shock dominated the mentality of those days. Unemployment was introduced to East Germany for the first time, and my mother lost her work as a bookkeeper. Fortunately, my mother rose to the challenge of surviving, rather than seeing herself as a victim. She used her knowledge and life experience to lease a local restaurant and turn it into a family business. I admired her strength and optimism, and at thirteen I joined in and helped her at the restaurant. I learned quickly that not giving up and working hard were the key factors to make the restaurant flourish.

With that knowledge I was already on my way to becoming a teacher. **(Scholarship judges hear excuses all the time about why people didn't achieve their goals; however, the disruptions caused by the fall of Communism and the Berlin Wall are a pretty darned good reason.)**

Different jobs after graduation not only gave me a little cash but also helped me to discover other essential skills, above all, patience and the ability to listen. My work at a rehabilitation program for disadvantaged mothers with children in Buckow, Germany gave me the insight on how crucial listening can be. The facility provided children between six months and sixteen years of age with a loving and learning environment. I was in charge of tutoring the school-aged children and helped them with diverse school assignments. My ability to listen to the children and their various problems helped them to trust me. As soon as the children opened up to me, they could more easily focus on their assignments and get their work done.

As a sales person in Fürstenwalde, Germany, seemingly a very different job from working at the rehabilitation center turned out to have similar experiences in store for me. Once again patience and listening, in this case to customers, made it easy to enjoy the work and help people with their purchases. Today, as a wife, student, peer tutor, and nanny, I use my listening skills more than ever. An open ear helps me to better understand the people around me. I know that patience and listening skills will bring me closer to becoming the best teacher I can possibly be. **(If she is currently a wife, student, tutor and nanny all at the same time, then I think she'll probably handle the demands of teaching without a great deal of difficulty.)**

The determination to master a language besides my native tongue adds another very important piece to my life's story. The English, Russian, and French I learned in school helped me to explore the world beyond German borders. Instead of reading about countries in Europe, I saved my meager salary and discovered them on my own. The ability to speak English opened a whole new world for me, since it is so widely spoken in Europe. The little money I made I used to experience the hospitality of Malta's people, the temperament of the Italians, and Switzerland's beauty. Without the confidence of speaking the language, I might have still visited these foreign places, but I would have missed out on the opportunity of getting to know the natives and their cultures. Hence, I enrolled as an Au Pair in the U.S. in order to perfect my English skills, and in 2000 I came to New York. Within a few months my language skills improved tremendously. I read a lot, watched TV shows, and learned from people's conversations. I was not afraid to make mistakes and encouraged everyone to correct me if I used incorrect terminology or grammar.

(I don't think I mentioned this in "Confessions," but the ability to speak multiple languages is always a great plus in scholarship applications, even if it's not mentioned in the criteria. Being multi-lingual always seems to impress people, and rightly so. Do you know any people who speak, say, three or more languages? If so, what's the first thing you say about them when you're describing them to others? Probably that they speak three or more languages. It's an impressive thing, because it shows commitment to learn difficult yet elective skills.)

After mastering conversational English, I took my studies a step further by advancing my writing skills as well. Besides the general required English writing classes at Dutchess Community College, I also enrolled in an American Contemporary Literature class. I also had the opportunity to improve my writing skills by participating in the Exploring Transfer Program at Vassar College last summer. The five-week Liberal Arts intensive writing program, co-taught by a Vassar professor and a Community College professor from different professional fields, shaped my writing as much as my critical thinking skills. The program offered full devotion to studying and learning, something I had not experienced before. I had always worked full time to afford tuition at DCC. Class discussions, literature readings, and demanding writing assignments at Vassar shaped and improved my writing style in ways I never thought possible. My determination to master the language helped me to go through the program and leave from it as a better writer.

After the intensity of Exploring Transfer I know anything is possible. I also know that if I went through the tough process of learning and mastering English, my future students, with my help, will be able to do so as well. I can fully relate to the obstacles they might face and help them overcome their possible fears about learning another language.

(Note the way this essay combines the author's early struggles -- in this case, with Communism and speaking English -- with her own mastery of these challenges, and again with the desire to help others. As I say repeatedly in the book -- struggle plus overcoming plus the

desire to help others is a time-tested and proven way to win scholarships.)

After adding English, I challenge myself once more by becoming a Spanish teacher. Since Americans already have the advantage of speaking English I choose Spanish to open an even broader world of opportunities for my future students. When learning Spanish, students will not only be able to explore English-speaking countries, but will have the tools to get to know the world of Spanish speakers as well. Instead of hearing about foreign places, I will give them the confidence to go out and discover for themselves. As a Spanish and German peer tutor, I am already working on helping students to learn another language and culture. The job makes me realize that teaching a language comes to me naturally. I cannot wait to teach an entire class and reach out to more than one student at a time. I am eager to encourage my future students to go and explore countries for themselves. It's priceless.

Equipped with all these pieces, I am now ready to acquire another vital part: the professional know- how of teaching. My life experiences and determination will be of little use if I do not strive to achieve the professional skills needed for a teaching occupation. I graduated from Dutchess Community College with an Associate's Degree and transferred this fall to SUNY New Paltz in Secondary Education with a major in Spanish. I am finally on the road to fulfill my childhood dream of becoming the magical teacher that I saw in Mrs. Maslowski. Although it took twenty years to reach this point in my life I know that every single one of them were positive and necessary. I know that in a communist country I would have never had the opportunities that I am offered now, and I also know that my educational journey is far from being over. There is still so much to learn and discover and I want to pass on some of the knowledge I obtained to my future students.

(A great job here bringing the conclusion full circle with the introduction regarding her late-bloomer status. Honestly, though, the essay revealed that her life has been so full of learning and involvement up to this point that I'd completely forgotten that she's talked about being a late bloomer in her introduction. Is there anything here to suggest that Caecilia would be anything other than a great investment for any scholarship committee to make? I think not.)

Shea Donato

Growing up in a house that included a criminal investigator as a mother, it is sometimes difficult for others to fathom why I have decided to walk down the same path towards criminal investigation and law enforcement. Living with a mother who was a member of law enforcement was akin to living with a human lie detector. During my teenage years I had to master the art of non-confrontation in order to avoid her interrogative techniques when I had stayed out past my curfew or did something else that I was not supposed to do. **(Very funny!)**

Despite these minor childhood infractions that I inevitably was busted for unless I managed to avoid the interrogation altogether, my mother and I could always talk to each other about crime and law enforcement issues on the same intellectual level. Even at the age of 15 I could understand my mother's concerns when the department she worked for adopted new protocols that did not mandate the use of bulletproof vests for patrol officers. Even though the nature of my mother's job as a homicide investigator did not include the same likelihood for high speed pursuits and the volatile situations that accompany them, I still easily understood the risks that came with what she did. It would be entirely accurate to say that I grew up in a law enforcement family.

The experiences that I had growing up with my mother being a law enforcement officer certainly influenced my own career goals. In a true rebellious teenager fashion, I formed goals to become a criminal trial attorney when I was in high school. I knew that my interests and passion were in the criminal justice system; I just was not sure whether I was going to follow in my mother's footsteps. I continued with my law school drive right up to my senior year in college, and I even took the Law School Admissions Test (LSAT) in February of my senior year of college. However, during that year I had begun to seriously question whether working as prosecuting attorney was the best place in the criminal justice system for me. By the time of my senior year, I was working part-time in a county attorney's office, and while I loved the work I was doing there, I became aware that the reason for that was merely the fact that it was working in the criminal justice system that I was enjoying. This seriously raised the question for me of whether I was enjoying the attorney side of it or just my place in the criminal justice system. It quickly became obvious for me that the career path I had originally shunned for the sake of my teenage rebellion was actually the very path I was perfect for. In the time that I worked at the attorney's office, it became more than obvious to me that I was much better with people than with files.

(There's a very sharp observation here that Shea makes, and most people his age don't make it. Shea has actually picked apart his own life and applied to it the scientific method. He observed his state of happiness in his job and is now trying to isolate the variable that causes the satisfaction: the position on the attorney side, or simply the idea of being in the criminal justice system. This is an extremely important call, and especially so in his case. Do you know how much money he would've spent via law school to become an attorney, only to get out and realize he wanted to be a cop? This is maturity in action, people -- being aware of all the forces and actions going on around you, dissecting and analyzing them into making the right decisions for yourself.)

In addition to the much-needed clarification on which career path would be ideal for me, I also received a very sobering look into the world of domestic violence and sexual assault in the context of the criminal justice system. The prosecutor I worked with focused mainly on these two types of cases, and I received a crash course on what I would argue to be the worst side of humanity. The very first jury trial that I was involved in is the one that I still remember clearly to this day. Our victim, a 5'2" partially disabled woman, was so terrified of the perpetrator, a 6'0" heavily built man, that she refused to testify in the courtroom. The judge agreed to allow the victim to testify through the phone. The victim agreed, and we literally had no idea where in the state, if she was even in the state anymore, she called in from. Even through the crackling of the phone connection, I could hear the victim's voice shaking. For me, that was a very eye-opening experience when it comes to the sheer amount of terror that this perpetrator had instilled in this poor woman. From then on, I had a very different outlook on life itself, but also my own place in the only system designed to protect society from these kinds of crimes. During my time in that office, the cases never seemed to end and every time I thought I had seen a case that was the worst of them all, another one came along that just elevated that standard. (And yet, while that would make most people run away, Shea decided to make it his life's work. That impresses guys like me, who sit behind a desk all day.)

For many, that kind of reality in the criminal justice system could cause cynicism and a sense of hopelessness. It's not easy to see these kinds of cases. However, for me, it only increased my resolve to work in the criminal justice field related to sexual assault and domestic violence crimes. I cannot think of a more blatant betrayal of trust then the kind that perpetrators of domestic violence and sexual assault inflict on their victims. It is the most severe form of violence that I can think of. Dr. Martin Luther King Jr. once said, "he who passively accepts evil is as much involved in it as he who helps to perpetrate it. He who accepts evil without protesting against it is really cooperating with it." I could not agree more with this statement. Dr. King, known almost exclusively for his work in civil rights, also highlighted the importance of standing up for what is right, and I fully agree with his sentiments. To state it bluntly, I believe it is incredibly wrong to inflict domestic violence or a sexual assault on anyone. My own observation of the incredibly devastating impact it has on the victims is more than enough to convince me of that. **(These last two sentences aren't necessary, since they obviously follow from everything he's already said, but that is a small ding on an otherwise very good essay.)**

This is what I hope to offer to the criminal justice system. I will be pursuing a Master's Degree in Criminal Justice Studies at the John Jay College of Criminal Justice at the City University of New York starting in the fall of 2007. I am currently serving as the project coordinator of the Helena Family Violence Council (HFVC) in the AmeriCorps VISTA (Volunteers in Service to America) program. I decided to spend one year dedicated to service in the area of domestic violence and sexual assault to make sure that this is what I really want to do. Nearly six months into my service term I am more sure than ever that this is what I plan to pursue after graduation from John Jay. Rather than pursuing a career based on whether or not it can offer me a six-digit salary, I have chosen to pursue a career based on what I personally believe. Like my mother, that resulted in a future career in law enforcement. I have always been sensitive to criticism of the criminal justice system because I know there are people like my mother serving in it. Every case that she manages to close is never what's reported on the news. Instead, we hear and read about the cases of police brutality or incompetence. The media is saturated with this kind of criticism, which while valid for the officers they are reporting on, fails to adequately represent the entire system. There are bad people in the system, which makes the criminal justice system just like every other government system out there. However, the involvement of people like my mother remind us that there are a lot of good people in it dedicated to keeping the people of their communities safe. I want to continue that and I plan to do everything I can to protect the community I end up living in from the perpetrators that seek to harm it.

(Well-done. Yet another example of a smart, dedicated guy following his heart to help people.

There's a recurring theme here....are you starting to see it?)

Pamela Escobar

As a child, I loved playing doctor with my mother, who suffered a severe neck injury in a car accident that left her paralyzed. I would trace my fingers along her stomach and back, wondering about the mysteries of the human body. I imagined that my handiwork had a healing power, and my mother indulged that fantasy. For years, I dreamed of becoming a famous doctor who would find a cure for spinal cord injuries that would restore my mother to her former self. Over time I realized that there would be no miraculous cure for her disability, which required careful and constant management if she were to thrive both physically and emotionally. My sister and I accompanied her to innumerable doctor visits, helped her with household chores, and assisted her with physical therapy exercises. These daily activities strengthened the intimacy between us and helped me view the world from a different perspective. The tedium, frustration, and rewards involved in taking care of a loved one with a chronic health condition, with its various demands and its constant uncertainty, have made me more sensitive to the ongoing needs of such patients. Now I want to become a doctor because I understand the powerful role a caring and knowledgeable physician can play in such a person's life. **(I love this introduction. In one extremely well-written paragraph, we learn about the childhood roots of Pamela's aspirations, the bond between her and her mother, the toll that a chronic condition takes on a family, and how it's affected her future plans. Phenomenal!)**

My goal as a doctor would be not only to heal my patients' physical ailments, but also to help them maintain good health by promoting wellbeing where they live. Community-based education programs can prevent widespread medical problems by disseminating knowledge through various social organizations. Instead of being a doctor who simply prescribes medicine to address a problem, I want to work in concert with my patients to empower them to take an active role in maintaining their own health. We now have sufficient medical information about heat disease, strokes, diabetes, AIDS, and certain forms of cancer to help educate the average layperson **(this is redundant -- say "layperson" or "the average person," but not "the average layperson." It's just a small quibble, but worth pointing out for instructional purposes.)** about how to prevent these maladies. Observing physicians treat my mother, I've noticed their various styles and methods. Some doctors enter a room with their eyes locked to the seemingly crucial information on their clipboards, mispronounce my mother's name, ask a few routine questions, prescribe medication, and assign a nurse to help see her out. Others rub her legs and back, ask about her physical therapy, question lifestyle choices that may affect her health, and explain several choices that may affect her well-being. This latter approach encourages patients to ask questions and reveal personal information that might impact their medical diagnosis. Rather than promoting silence, these doctors welcome a partnership with their patients in the healing process. **(I sense that Pamela is writing with some pent-up passion here. Can you tell which kind of doctor she wants to be?)**

I envision my role as physician as healer and educator, a professional who serves as a resource to her patients. Physicians need the assistance of their patients to prescribe the proper treatment of an ailment. Helping my mother in her physical exercises, I appreciate her influence in my pursuit of medicine. Her odyssey through the medical profession has shown me the importance of treating patients in a holistic context. This approach not only is ethically significant in its focus on respecting a patient's human dignity, but also is indispensable in increasing awareness of preventive medicine and community education. **(Very clearly stated, and very easy to agree with. Listen to what she's saying here about the importance of helping other people -- is there, so far, any reason under the sun that she would not deserve scholarship money?)**

I plan to double major in human biology and community health. As a freshman in the eight-year medical program, these two majors allow me the opportunity to learn the scientific aspect of medicine as well as a population-based view of health. **(Sounds like an aggressive plan of study, so she gets points from me for taking on a large challenge. Are you taking on a big challenge with your college plans? If yes, it's good to say so, like Pamela does.)** These clinical areas of study allow the flexibility to respond to and anticipate changes in heath care and to incorporate these changes within the community in order to better the human condition.

Establishing a network between service and opportunity, I am deeply passionate about my involvement in graduate research and volunteering. Adopting a vision of a greater good for my Hispanic community and satiating my cultural curiosity, I volunteer as a translator in a homeless medical clinic off campus. The ability to communicate across the language barrier not only further promotes and facilitates diagnosis and treatment, but also preventative medicine and community education. These experiences enhance what I learn in the classroom and apply it within the context of people's lives. Gleaning skills as a student as well as a physician, these experiences provide a means for me to continue my dedication to service in a clinical setting and find the mentors that will guide me into becoming a socially responsible doctor.

This essay isn't particularly long, but it's an example of why a great essay doesn't have to be. Read back through it and you'll see that no words are wasted; every sentence is important and contains ideas critical and relevant to the essay. It takes the average scholarship applicant 10 pages to communicate what Pamela just communicated in 2-1/2 pages. Excellent job.

Debra Pachucki

These days, it seems that education majors are a dime a dozen, and the same can be said of their responses to the kind of teacher they would like to be and why. **(Wow, it sounds like Debra has been a scholarship judge lately. I think she's 100% right!)** I'm not sure if my reasons can be considered unique, astute, or even impressive, but they are sincere, and that's good enough for me. I want to be a teacher because I possess a degree of intelligence that I feel morally obligated to share, because I feel a natural empathy toward young adults dealing with the "storm and stress" of adolescence, and because the time I've spent as a student has led me to feel confident that I can be equally contributive to education in the form of a leader. I know this career path doesn't pay well, but I've always measured wealth in terms of spirit and not in dollars and cents. **(It's a good thing, because she's right about teacher pay! Seriously, though, as I mentioned in the book, the notion that money isn't one's top priority is one that resonates well with the committee.)**

Along my educational career, my own teachers have repeatedly told me that "knowledge is power." And in the words of Spiderman's Uncle Ben, "with great power comes great responsibility." (A note here: although I mention in the book not to quote pop culture, I actually think this is a clever and intentionally humorous combination of quotes.) Although the first quote comes from respected education professionals and the latter comes from the fictitious kin of a comic superhero, I believe that both quotes are equally meaningful and go hand-in-hand in terms of educational pedagogy. When I first came to realize that my teachers were right, and that knowledge really is power, I was a twenty three year old college student who quickly began to imagine the money I could stand to make if I were to become an executive administrator or a lawyer. Confident that I was smart enough to do it, I registered for a criminal law course, intending for it to be my launching pad into the world of professional success and financial endowment. It wasn't long before I dropped the course, due to an overwhelming (and seemingly illogical) feeling that to use my academic talents so selfishly just wasn't right for me. Yes, I am smart. I could use my intelligence to acquire a great paying job, get a fancy car, and finally afford to shop in stores whose names do not end in the word "mart." But would it be fulfilling? Frustratingly, no. As Uncle Ben's words of wisdom continued to flutter through my mind, I couldn't help but to realize that for me, the best thing I could do with my intelligence would not be to use it for money, but to use it to give America's youth a better chance at acquiring a similar intelligence for themselves. **(Again, this spirit of putting service** over material wealth is one that committees seem to enjoy, so it's smart to communicate this in your essay.)

At this point, you might be wondering, "Well, why America's youth? Why not be a doctor, and use your intelligence to better the countless sick and ailing?" Or, "How about becoming a veterinarian, and assisting animals in need?" The answer is simple: I can relate to the struggles of teenage life better than I can to the struggles of the unhealthy and/or to nonhuman species. I believe that a large part of being an effective teacher is being able to extend one's services beyond academics and into overall wellbeing. I was always a bright student, but had more than my fair share of difficulty as a teenager in the late 1990s. I am a victim of sexual abuse, I was raised in a dangerous urban environment, and I am a survivor of prejudice, jealousy, and ridicule by those who were unlike me. I am not bitter or resentful of any of the things that have made me who I am today, and I continually feel that the best way to rectify these injustices is to turn them into a means by which to help others avoid or overcome such common obstacles associated with growing up. I can honestly say that I truly care and understand what a lot of adolescents go through, and I believe that such care and understanding can truly benefit my students in a very fundamental way. **(This paragraph reflects a couple different pieces of advice that you read about in the "Confessions" book -- the idea of turning your hardships into motivation for bettering yourself and helping others, as well as the portrayal of your hardships as something you don't want pity for.)**

On the opposite end of the spectrum, academics is in fact the very core of education, and as one who has established a high degree of intellect as a student in the classroom, I am ready to continue my love of the teaching and learning process on the other side of the desk, so to speak. (OK, in all fairness...probably no need for Debra to keep repeating herself about her intellect and academic excellence. Confidence is good, but we get it already). I am confident that the knowledge and wisdom I've acquired thus far has prepared me for a role in educational leadership, and I welcome the challenges associated with educational theories and practices in the 21st century. They say a teacher's job is never done, and for that, I am grateful. For I can't begin to imagine the static boredom that must be associated with the feeling that one has accomplished everything they've wanted to, with nothing else to aspire toward. **(This is a unique insight; one of the benefits of teaching most often cited is that every day is a new challenge. I am not a teacher myself, but I agree that this must be true, and despite the pay, teachers definitely have this going for them: they don't have to plop themselves down in front of a computer screen every day with** minimal human interaction. **This is a point that a lot of students don't think about when they choose a career in which staring into a computer screen is a primary activity.)**

With this being said, I foresee myself as being an effective, encouraging teacher. One who understands her students, and one who raises the bar for her students in an effort to help them strive to be the best that they can be. I will always welcome humor and unique ideas in my classroom, but will never tolerate disrespect toward myself or other students. I will encourage free thinking and individuality, and will do all I can to maintain a thriving learning environment for all who frequent my classroom. I will welcome student interests, and rely on them to help motivate and spark learning, not discourage it. These are the things I have lived my life by, and are the things I believe everyone is entitled to have.

(Admirable thoughts, one and all.)

Sure, by becoming a teacher, I am committing myself to an infinite era of student loan repayments, Ramen Noodle dinners, and a wardrobe comprised of clearance items collected from discount superstores. But those things don't scare me! In fact, they make me smile. And once those fleeting thoughts have passed, I'm left with a wealth of opportunity, experience, and never-ending accomplishments to look forward to. Why do I want to be a teacher, you ask? Because I'm looking forward to reaping endless rewards through the career of my choice. I'm just not looking for them in the form of a five figure check.

Well-said, although I assume she means's a five-figure monthly check, since even our lowest-paid teachers make over $10,000 per year! Overall, a very straightforward and inspiring essay. I don't doubt Debra will make a great teacher someday.

Tiffany Vu

Medicine is undoubtedly one of the most significant and needed professions in the world. Regardless of where you go, there will always be people in need of medical attention especially in underserved and underprivileged areas. These regions are where I anticipate practicing medicine. Health is the most important basic need; without health, there would not be life. My aspirations to become a pediatrician originally stemmed from my experiences as a volunteer and were later strengthened through clinical experience. I still remember one of my first experiences as a pediatrics volunteer several years ago. **(A very nice and thorough, yet concise, introduction. In a few short sentences, we learn about Tiffany's appreciation for the medical profession, her future plans to help those who need medical care the most, and that she's already been doing volunteer work in this regard. I'm ready to hear more! And if you'll allow me a quick tangent, that's rarely the case -- the case that I'm ready to hear more. Most of the time, the writer's first paragraph is boring or just plain bad, and I really don't want to hear any more. If you can get past the first paragraph of your essay leaving the committee wanting more, you're doing better than 90 percent of your counterparts.)**

I was a new volunteer at The HSC Pediatric Center in Washington, D.C., a rehabilitative and transitional center for children with chronic illnesses and disabilities. Ashley greeted me with a captivating smile as if I could not have arrived too soon. We caught up with each other while playing with the Candyland board game. While Ashley showed me how to play Candyland my mind drifted back to the day I met her. That day, the nurse had directed me to a little girl lying on her stomach, an IV attached to her wrist. I noticed that she could maneuver her bed like a wheel chair. She inquired if I was her new playmate as she tried to navigate around the wide doors of her room. I helped her with her battle with the door and wondered how she could be so enthusiastic in her condition.

Ashley had little control over her body except her arms. She was African-American and beautiful, particularly because of her enthusiasm and hopeful outlook on life. The memory faded and I refocused my attention on her little blue man reaching Candy Castle before mine. I never forgot what she said next: "Sometimes I am lonely because it's hard to play by myself but then you come in to play and I am happy we are friends." At 11 years old, Ashley unknowingly gave me an understanding that part of a physician's duty includes immense compassion and commitment. The last thing she needed was pity. She needed hope. Physicians, nurses, and volunteers gave it to her daily encouraging her to create her own happiness despite her condition. These new beginnings as a volunteer showed me why becoming a health care professional is very necessary. **(That's a poignant story, and I like the details, especially the quote. It's sad and moving. If you're describing a similar incident in your essay, take your lead from how Tiffany doesn't use 6-8 sentences to explain Ashley's attitude and outlook; she lets Ashley, in one moving quote, do it all.)**

I volunteered at several different places including a few hospitals but there was one very distinct memory that I still think about today. After several months at INOVA Fairfax Hospital, I still remember one particular day on the oncology unit.

"What am I going to do without her?" a patient's tearful husband asked Eric Cohen, the Oncology Nurse Educator. The man's wife was a victim of metastasized breast cancer that had spread to her liver. Just 10 minutes prior, I helped Nurse Cohen and the husband take care of the patient because she was vomiting. Things calmed down and she wheezed as she slept. Nurse Eric explained how her family should consider quality of life care if the patient did not respond to therapy. The husband asked, "How long does she have if we take her off chemotherapy?" Eric replied, "I am not sure, but at most a few months." The husband sobbed, "What am I going to do without her? She is all I have." I saw the look in his eyes, the look of desperation and heartbreak and I broke down. While Eric was trying to console him, I turned to look out the window and wondered why I was crying. It was the first time I was hit by the inescapable reality faced by health care providers, loved ones and patients. I looked at the patient felt death seeping in through the cracks of the window and under the doorway. I felt powerless but now I recognize that death is a part of the profession as well as success. **(Another excellent anecdote complete with quotes even more poignant than the first. But lest you think the strength of this paragraph lies in the tear-jerker quotes, it's not just that. Those quotes serve a purpose: as Tiffany goes on to explain, they illustrate how she began to understand that, for doctors, death is part of the job. A mature observation.)**

Eric briefed me on the patient's condition and bluntly explained, "I don't think she is going to make it. Metastasized cancer is different from a car accident or a heart attack. Those patients can get better but this is the best she will ever be. She is going to die from this cancer." The physician mentioned trying to request a Do Not Resuscitate order. As there are many successes in the world of medicine, I recognize that there will also be rough times, failures, and deaths. The best that any physician can do is to provide the best care he or she can - and that always includes compassion and support.

Eric ensured me that her physicians, nurses and even I could make it more comforting for her even if she could not be cured. The fact that the husband has a chance to say, "I love you and I'll miss you," and she will be able to say it back to him is valuable. Death does not have to be fought with pain and fear. It can be made into a more peaceful passage with the support and help from physicians and health care providers. **(Tiffany is putting together a wickedly effective set of paragraphs here. Like a boxer putting together punches that really hit you in the gut, Tiffany's doing the same thing here. But remember that the excellence of the essay comes in the fact that she's using them to illustrate the things she's learned from these emotional experiences.)**

I have had many experiences as a volunteer and currently as a medical assistant for years. I worked at an adult and pediatric asthma, allergy and immunotherapy medical office in Washington, D.C. I was trained as a medical assistant qualified to administer various injections such as allergy immunotherapy, tetanus, influenza virus vaccine, immune globulin as well as many other types of injections. My job required knowledge of the correct dosage according to weight, size and age of the person and past medical allergic history. The hands-on practice I gained as a medical assistant in facilitating efficient screening of blood pressure, pulmonary function tests and allergy skin prick tests and intradermal testing on top of interacting directly with the patients is valuable to helping me later succeed as a physician. But the most essential experiences that I have had on the job are the ones that require quick thinking and acting.

It was the first time I saw a patient experiencing anaphylaxis, a potentially fatal allergic reaction. He rushed back into the office an hour after he received his allergy shots and started tearing his shirt off. He was wheezing and had hives all over his body. I took one look at it and felt for an instance that it was my fault and that I must have done something wrong. But I quickly reorganized my thoughts and raced for the doctor. I found the epinephrine and injected the adult dosage into him while Dr. Carrgel explained the side effects of epinephrine to him. Then I set up the nebulizer and had him stay on it for 20 minutes while watching over him as he slowly got better. It was a stressful moment for me specially because it was the first time I saw a strong reaction to one of my injections but I quickly did what I needed to do and everything worked out. There have been a handful of these types of reactions since working at the office and the experience in helping the patient recover gives me a very important perspective in medicine. It is always vital to remain collective and be able to make priorities quickly but efficiently in emergency situations. **(Wow, that's impressive. This paragraph adds to the essay by showing that Tiffany isn't only a passive, empathetic companion to her patients, but also a woman of action who stays cool under pressure. At this point, I'm ready to vote for her as the winner. Either that, or it's going to take some kind of Herculean effort by another applicant to unseat Tiffany.)**

I think that the most prevalent problem facing healthcare today is the lack of medical attention in many areas, specifically the inner cities and even more so in rural regions. There are also many uninsured families and individuals who need medical attention, but cannot afford it. People could be drawn to medicine for many other reasons but the one thing I care about is practicing in an underserved or underprivileged area to better improve their health. Thus, I am matriculating at Lake Erie College of Osteopathic Medicine in Bradenton, Florida. As an aspiring osteopathic physician, I feel that with my training I would be able to improve this situation by choosing to practice in any of the disadvantaged urban or rural regions of America. It is my hope and goal to improve the quality of health and the lives of children in underserved regions. I want to practice pediatric medicine because through my volunteering experience and desires, I have found that we need to try to treat children and teach prevention at a young age particularly in an area where they need it most. **(Not only that, but it's probably a good way to get a lot of her student loans paid back for free, too. OK, that was a digression -- the get-all-the-money-you-can, advocate side of me took over for a minute. But obviously, if the rest of the essay wasn't enough, the spirit of community service and helping people is shining through here, and everyone on a committee loves to hear that.)**

For a few months between 2001 and 2002, I shadowed Dr. Theresa Flack at the Arlington Pediatric Center for underprivileged children whose family incomes fall below 200% of the Federal Poverty Line. This was the first experience that opened my eyes to the reality of the dire necessities of free clinics and the value of being a selfless and compassionate physician. I hope to become this type of physician that can incorporate the philosophy of osteopathic medicine and facilitate in an area where there is a physician shortage. Providing medical care for those who need it the most, yet are incapable of finding the resources or finances, is one of the primary issues facing healthcare today in America. As a physician,

I would aim to emphasize my responsibility to the community, as well as to the improvement and well-being of that community.

These experiences and observations have taught me that it is essential for physicians to have endurance, commitment, dedication, and compassion. It can be incredibly tough to watch families bear so much pain or young children struggling to live a normal life. Ashley and others after her, like the cancer patient have reinforced my passion and furthered my understanding of the devotion that is required of medical doctors. As an aspiring physician, I am ready to take on the challenges in making a life more bearable, in the possibility of saving a life, or for that fleeting glimpse of hope.

First-rate, from start to finish. Enough said.

Erica deBardeleben

Black America is being sedated by the media and pop culture in ways that misrepresent and mislead the community. **(Wow! That is one ballsy, take-no-prisoners opening statement! Do tell us more!)** Hip-hop artists have glamorized the harsh realities of the impoverished amongst us, black political leaders and intellectuals more readily support a "race-less" future, and the pro-black visionaries of yesteryear have been made complacent by the codification of anti-discriminatory policy. These groups, in consciousness or not, have turned the desperate condition of black America into an "invisible community"—a forgotten wasteland of vice, addiction, anger, and limited mobility—all while the media provides them with celebrity status and an unapproachable demeanor that neither inspires nor mobilizes those whom they claim to represent. That having been said, I am frustrated (you don't say?) by the marginalization of impoverished blacks and am tired of the larger community's silence on the issues that are slowly but surely perpetuating generational hopelessness.

(Man, talk about a hot start! I love this so far -- Erica's got strong opinions and she's going to tell you all about them. I hope that she proposes her own solutions and direction later on in the essay. Let's read on...)

The issues surrounding black America have long preoccupied my thoughts. Having grown up in a "broken" home, but raised far from it, I was provided with the rare opportunity of experiencing hopelessness but not becoming a part of it. My bi-racial teenage mother, caught in an abusive relationship with my alcoholic father, sent me to live with my white grandmother—a woman who taught me that the only definition that matters is the one you create for yourself. I recognize that in today's racially blended society, the circumstances surrounding my upbringing are not uncommon. It is unique, however, in that it is solely responsible for my perception of life and society. **(She's right, I suppose -- being biracial isn't unique, but the subjects she's bringing up are seldom written about, and even more rare is the perspective she brings due to her interesting upbringing. I am all ears here, eager to read more...)**

I have always felt that my life is a living dichotomy. I grew up in either the "white" world of Ann Arbor or the "black" world of Detroit; a single parent household or double. My childhood could be described as happy, carefree and privileged or terrorized by alcoholism, dysfunction, and near poverty. Academically, I was either overwhelmingly passionate about my work or absolutely unmotivated to pursue subjects of which I had no interest. I attended an all black college and then substantiated that experience by going to a graduate school where students of color where few and far between. Professionally, I began my adult life as a teacher in one of North Philadelphia's toughest ghettos. My next position, in drastic contrast, was as a consultant with a prestigious educational consulting organization with strong ties to the Bush Administration. Since I live my life along clearly defined lines, my nature compels me to take a strong stand in defense of what I feel is right. It is nearly impossible for me to straddle the fence on issues of social, political and economic importance and I always find myself in support of the underserved, the disenfranchised, and the marginalized amongst us. **(I agree, Erica has certainly seen "both sides of the coin," if you will, in many arenas. Let's hear the meat of the essay!)**

The stark contrasts that I have experienced in life taught me many truths about both myself and the world that we live in. The most important lesson, upon which I plan to base my body of work in film and electronic media, is that having varied and enriching experiences allows us to make sense of ourselves and the world around us. If one were to take this tenet and apply it to impoverished black America, one would see that the problem lies neither in victimization nor lack of motivation, but instead in the ignorance that they unknowingly carry. This community, reliant upon cable television, radio, and other forms of media to provide them with information, is being manipulated and exploited by networks that claim to be their representatives to the mainstream. **(I like it! There's no hesitation whatsoever in Erica's message here, and I also like how she slides her career aspiration of making films right into one of her sentences without missing a beat.)**

I base my assertions upon the personal and professional experiences that I have had working in disenfranchised, predominately black neighborhoods. As a Teach for America teacher, unlike most of my peers, I chose to live in the same North Philadelphia neighborhood in which I worked. I witnessed more of what it means to be frustrated by limited mobility then, than I ever have in my life. Most of my students had never ventured beyond the six-block radius of their neighborhood, and emulated the things that they heard on television and the radio as ultimate truths—a problematic norm that I would like to change. **(It's rare, but wonderful, when the essay writer actually teaches you something in the course of reading their essay, or at least gives you a different perspective. I like to think I'm a forward-thinking adult who** probably does more contemplating of society's problems than the average Joe, but I'd never even considered this angle before -- the angle that students from the roughest ghettos take the news they hear on TV and radio to be the ultimate truth. I would've thought the opposite: that they'd mistrust, often to a fault, media messages. In any case, Erica just made me think a little. Thanks, Erica!)

Despite being an effective and highly motivated teacher, I became "burnt-out" by the seemingly endless drama that kept my students from focusing on changing the cycles of oppression. I then decided to focus my energies on changing the system by entering the educational policy world. As a consultant, I hoped to share the practices and insight that I gained while in the classroom to improve struggling schools. This ideal, however, proved in vain. I found that the educational system, as is the case in others, is so heavily bogged down by bureaucracy that its major players feel no connection to its true purpose. I also found that many organizations espousing to improve the system by working outside of it do so either for profit or for status and rarely out of sincere agency. In essence, I have grown quite cynical of and jaded by the system. My heart bleeds for those who are trapped in it. After of all of this, I've decided that I'd like to study film and electronic media. Why? First and foremost, I want to become a major player in the creation and dissemination of mass media to underserved peoples. If I were able to manipulate imagery in an effective and compelling fashion, I might be able to present information in ways that allow the people to transcend complacency. I want to make movies that inspire people and make the world a better place to live in—that heighten awareness and compel people to change their lives for the better. I have also enjoyed a hobby in film, writing and photography for some time now, and would like to merge my passions with my talents so that I can feel ownership over my career. (Again, an extremely impressive paragraph idea fueled by creative ideas. A teacher doesn't like what she sees in the education world yet still wants to help, so she gets the idea to go study film and media to get her message out there. Would you have thought of that if you were in her shoes? I wouldn't have.)

During my senior year in college, I was part of a team that developed a short documentary called, "Femcees: Women in Hip-Hop". Working on this film was one of the most rewarding experiences that I have ever had. I really challenged myself and my group to work in ways that would merge the women's stories with their "inner-selves" by creating complete images within each frame; that is to say that I wanted the surroundings to tell as much of the story as the subject. Though our novice piece had its imperfections, the response that we received was all in high praise. So strong was our body of work that even after our screening at Spelman, we were invited to show "Femcees" at Temple University and the 2nd Atlanta Women of Color International Film Festival. Even there, our audience felt the importance of the messages that we were relaying and supported us in continuing on with the work. My experience with "Femcees" proved to me the power in film. Doing more and better work has constantly been on my mind since.

(Awesomely bold and focused, from start to finish. Congrats!)

Edward Thomas

Could there be a world where nearly five million people perish as a result only three brutal civil conflicts in as many years? Could there be a world where international humanitarian law provides a framework lacking enforcement, to protect women, children, the elderly and infirmed, from such atrocities? Could there be a world where the international community, able to guarantee the safety of civilians with only minimal economic and political costs, chooses instead to stand by idly? Could there be a world where, looking for signs of progress, one only finds disappointment? A world where, a decade prior, the picture was alarmingly the same? The tragic answer to all these is 'yes.' **(That's definitely a downer of an introduction, but I'm interested in hearing the details, so I'll call it a good intro.)**

Consider each and every year over the last decade and a half – be it 1994, 1999, 2004, or 2006 – and one is easily reminded of the horrors of Somalia, Rwanda, Georgia, Bosnia, Kosovo, Sierra Leone, Cote d'Ivoire, Sri Lanka, and so many other civil conflicts. In the last three years, the Democratic Republic of the Congo, Iraq, and Sudan/Darfur have become the newest in a frighteningly long list.

Yet the power to act is clearly within reach. The last three years have seen a tremendous flurry of activity within the international community. The global adoption of the 'Responsibility to Protect' doctrine, reforms at the United Nations' Department of Peacekeeping Operations, and the inauguration of the International Criminal Court are all indications that the world may finally be willing to stand behind the oft-cited expression, "Never Again." It is a cause worthy of the greatest efforts, for the rewards to the global community are tremendous; the costs of inaction are unimaginable. Knowing this, my aspirations in life are clear. **(OK, Edward has established himself here, for now, as a big thinker who has his mind on big problems. That, we like to hear. Let's see how he plans to make a difference.)**

Currently in my third year at Trinity College in the University of Toronto, I am studying toward an Honours Bachelor of Arts degree, with a Joint Specialist in International Relations and Peace and Conflict Studies. This is a highly competitive programme, accepting fewer than 25 students per year (and less than 5 per year into the Joint Specialist stream). Within the programme's curriculum, I have chosen a self-designed thematic focus on 'peacebuilding and post-conflict development,' as well as undertaking independent research on protracted ethnic conflict and peacebuilding in the Caucasus. I have published first-author pieces in the Canadian Undergraduate Journal for Development Studies, and have assisted with authoring pieces in International Journal and in World Bank Group publication series, as well as having been a guest lecturer at Trinity College. Related to my studies, I am pursuing linguistic competencies in French, German, and Russian. **(Clearly, Edward is backing up his lofty ideals with concrete actions. He's cracked a top-flight program, writing in respected journals, and, by the way, learning three languages. Remember the book's advice on letting us know when you speak multiple languages? Well-done, Edward.)**

Broadly speaking, my research interests are centred on the human security aspects of international development. Thematically, this includes: the causes of inter- and intra-group conflict, particularly civil war and identity- conflict; the international dimensions of civil conflict, particularly the relationship between intra-state conflict and regional instability; and, issues pertaining to contemporary conflict prevention, peacebuilding, and peacekeeping. Pertaining to the last issue, I am particularly drawn toward an interest in the changing nature of peacekeeping, as it has evolved from its traditional model toward a conceptualization more centrally focused on stabilization and peace enforcement operations. Regionally, my research has been primarily focused on the Caucasus, the Horn of Africa and north-central Africa (particularly Sudan/Darfur-Chad-Central African Republic), and the Great Lakes Region of Africa. Outside of the realm of human security, I have conducted research on issues pertaining to international relations history (i.e. the end of European 'concert diplomacy' ca. the late-19th century),contemporary global governance (such as the changing nature of North-South relations vis-à-vis the development agenda), contemporary African politics (notably a paper on the rationality of personal rule), and general anthropology (including a paper on the discourses surrounding Native American gambling, and a paper on the responses of African literature to post-colonial discourse). **(I would've rather seen Edward talk solely about his paper topics, rather than on labeling them with terms such as "contemporary global governance," "general anthropology" and the like -- this is a move away from specifics and toward vagueness.)**

While maintaining a GPA of 3.73 (out of 4.0) and standing on the Dean's Honours List, I spend a great deal of my time outside of the classroom. I have recently joined the Canadian Forces as an Officer attached to the Governor General's Horse Guards, an Armoured Reconnaissance unit in the Primary Reserves. My military training is heavily focused around the provision of humanitarian aid and security within the context of peacekeeping, peace enforcement, and stabilization operations. I am also working as a Research Assistant at the Munk Centre for International Studies in the University of Toronto, wherein I work with the Executive Director on a project that is making measurable strides in attempting to bridge the daunting policy gap between international development and the role of multinational corporations. I am also a long-standing volunteer with Médecins Sans Frontières / Doctors Without Borders, assisting with recruitment and human resources for field missions, as well as with fundraising and donor relations. For the last eight months, I have served as the security policy analyst for the Canadian arm of a leading international think tank and student advocacy group focused on the humanitarian crisis in Darfur region of Sudan. **(That's one hell of a kicker onto the end of an already very strong essay: military training, security policy analyst and a longtime volunteer for Doctors Without Borders. Again, as it relates to the GMS concepts, Edward is doing an excellent job providing details of his dedication to his stated cause and also showing his passion for his subject matter.)**

I remain dedicated to assisting those within and around my University's community, through a number of extra-curricular involvements. These include holding the inaugural position as the Trinity College Peace and Conflict Studies Peer Counselor, and as a volunteer with the City of Toronto / University of Toronto's collaborative community food and clothing bank. Moreover, I am currently serving a second term as the Treasurer for the Peace and Conflict Society, which represents the students in this program at the University of Toronto. Related to this involvement, I sit on the executive of a student-run committee tasked with organizing an annual three-day conference on topics in conflict studies. This workshop series, entirely student organized, brings together scholars, practitioners and students, the aim being the building of an international forum on conflict prevention, mediation and resolution. Our 2007 conference, focusing on conflict prevention, will include on its speaker list individuals such as the former Deputy Secretary General of the United Nations, the president of the International Crisis Group, and a senior intelligence officer attached to MONUC (the United Nations peacekeeping operation in the Democratic Republic of the Congo). Unrelated personal interests include music and sports (guitar, squash and ball hockey), literature (particularly 19th century European and 20th century African), and aviation. I concurrently hold my Recreational Pilot Permit and Private Pilot License with over 330 hours of experience on a variety of different types of aircraft. I am nearly finished training toward my Instrument Rating and Commercial Pilots License. At age 16, I was the youngest licensed pilot in Canada. **(This is usually where I say, "unrelated personal interests don't belong in an essay!" and I stand by** that statement regarding the literature, sports, etc. However, the fact that he was the youngest licensed pilot in Canada is definitely a unique accomplishment that's worth mentioning, in the state champion/Eagle Scout arena that I refer to in the book.)

During the coming eighteen months, in addition to my regular academic and military studies, I plan to attend the Peace Operations Summer Institute at the Royal Military College, as well as completing a certificate in Refugee Studies and Management from York University. Following the completion of my degree, I intend to expand upon my involvement with the Canadian Forces, by pursuing a deployment of six to nine months (2008-2009) with a United Nations peacekeeping operation, likely in Haiti or South Sudan. Following this deployment, I will pursue a twelve-month internship (2009-2010) with the International Crisis Group in Brussels, Belgium. After this internship, I will pursue a Master's degree in War Studies at King's College London. As well, I expect to complete the certificate program in International Humanitarian Assistance at Uppsala Universiteit, Sweden. These graduate studies would likely be completed by 2012, at which point I aim to work with the United Nations' Department of Peacekeeping Operations, focusing on bringing my academic and practical knowledge of human security together with a career focused on international development and conflict prevention/mediation/resolution.

Edward has it all planned out, doesn't he? The committee does indeed like a man with a plan, and he's got years of details built into his. Overall, a great essay that really demonstrates the values and commitment this guy has to his own personal and professional vision. Extremely well-done.

Alexandra Avila

To know why college is so important to me, it is necessary to know a little bit about me. Although born in Virginia, I lived around 10 years in South America before returning to the U.S. when I was 14. We decided to come back because of a series of hardships in Ecuador including my father's death, the economic collapse of the country, and several volcanoes erupting all around, which were making it quite hard to breathe! My father's death, of course, had a huge impact on my life. It shattered many things I took for granted. Despite the fact that he was very sick ever since I could remember, I guess I expected he would always find a way to cheat death. I spent much of my childhood taking care of him. He was in and out of the hospital ever since I was a toddler. I would come home from school to help him with his medication or to clean out his surgery wounds. His death left me hurt and vulnerable for a long time, but it also made me more determined to get ahead in life and to try to be someone my father would have been proud of. He fought very hard, working two full-time jobs and leaving his family behind in Paraguay, so that he could complete his education in the United States. For me to graduate from college was always a big dream for him and I would want to make him proud of me wherever he is. **(The writing still is a bit rambling here, but it does foreshadow an interesting story, so I'm sticking with it.)**

So going to college you might say has been my life ambition for many years now. I also want to be the first woman in my family to go to graduate from college, hopefully with a Master's Degree. I have seen all the hardships that my mom has had to go through because of my grandparents' decision for her not to go to college because she was a girl. She has been the breadwinner most of my life and it has not been easy for her. I want to have a good profession to give back to her some of what she has given to me and to be able to take care of her when she needs it. **(Fair enough -- a noble wish for anyone to aspire to. Let's hear more...)**

Since we lost all of our savings when the economy in Ecuador collapsed, we had only our suitcases and $3,000 when we decided to come back to the United States. This was very hard for me at first, as I had been used to a different lifestyle, but now I am glad because of all the opportunities I have had here. Living in the United States changed my life very much. Coming here made me mature and grow up faster and learn to fend for myself. It was very traumatic to leave behind my friends, a close-knit community, and everything I had known for all of my life and come to a strange new place were everything was so absolutely different from what I had been used to. The first several months I cried every single night. I felt miserable and all alone and did not think I would ever get used to living here. The experience made me realize how tough life can be, but it also inspired me to work harder, and it made me appreciate even more everything I had once taken for granted. **(I would like to have heard more about the collapse of Ecuador's economy, because I have no knowledge of this and I don't know what she's referring to. Otherwise, though, a good-enough description of a tough beginning in the U.S.)**

Although now very happy to live here, the life I had in Ecuador continues to be a very important part of who I am and the field of study I have chosen. I lived in the mountains, but within hours could be in a cloud forest, tropical jungle, or the Galapagos Islands. I learned to love and appreciate nature, looking forward to weekend outings to learn more about the diverse flora and fauna. I became worried about what pollution and overpopulation were doing to these beloved places and began to aspire to founding a non-profit organization dedicated to environment conservation, preserving what we have for future generations. College is my path to making this dream come true. At Hood, where I study, I am combining courses in Biology with Environmental Science and Policy, and since my long term goals include overseeing the administration of a nonprofit organization, I must later take courses in management and fund-raising.

In addition to my regular course load, I am helping Dr. Eric Kindahl who is the Assistant Professor of Biology and Director of Environmental Science and Policy Program at Hood. We are monitoring amphibians within the Catoctin Mountain area of Maryland in order to assess factors that affect population size. I helped search for, catch, weigh and measure mostly Redback, Leadback, Slimy, and Two-lined salamanders, although other amphibians such as the American Toad were also collected, weighed and measured.

I have tried to do many other things to help me achieve my goals. This past summer I was an Intern at Smithsonian Environmental Research Center in Edgewater, Maryland where I conducted field ecological research in the Chesapeake Bay, working primarily on the establishment of a new project using Crassostrea virginica hatchery oyster spat to conduct tests of oyster growth and disease in the Rhode, West, and South Rivers. **(Very interesting, and a good example of how to describe exactly the sort of work you're doing or have done, rather than**

glossing over the details with vague labels.) I participated in meetings with local watermen associations, learned from the Chesapeake Bay Foundation's Discovery Village about oyster spat rearing procedures, and had to obtain and transport old oyster shells to serve as clutches for the oyster spat to strike on. I also helped to set up three preliminary tanks in the Wet Lab to cultivate the oyster spat under different salinity and density conditions, monitoring the tanks to determine which conditions seemed to produce more and better spat, and transferred larger specimens to the river to repopulate oyster reefs. **(Although I didn't know, and still don't know, what oyster spat is, it's interesting to hear the details of what she's doing. I realize that there may be some conflict between a couple of items in the Book: the part about being specific and giving details, and the part about doing your best not to talk in such technical detail that you are "over the committee's head," if you will. When in doubt, err on the side of detail. Even in this case where I don't understand exactly what's going on with Alexandra's research, I can still tell that the part she's playing in the research is important and not simply grunt work.)**

Other tasks included inputting and analyzing data collected on the factors that affect oyster spat growth, and giving two presentations of research project to diverse audiences. In addition I helped to write an article for local association paper and I also helped out in the blue crab biology project, testing the feasibility of using hatchery-reared juvenile crabs to replenish the declining stock of blue crabs in the Bay and helped with monitoring program tracking species composition and abundances of fish and invertebrates in the Rhode River subestuary.

Currently I am participating in the Spring 2006 Coastal Semester at Hood College which encompasses, among other things, study visits at the University of Florida's Seahorse Key Laboratory, the Harbor Branch Oceanographic Institute, the Mote Marine Laboratory Center for Tropical Research, and the Chesapeake Biological Laboratory. Among other things, so far we investigated the hard shell clam aquaculture industry; learned from some of the top research scientists in marine science; visit the captain of a submersible; received lectures on coral reefs and endocrine disruptors, coastal oceanography and coastal community ecology; visited the Smithsonian Marine Station; investigated the Everglades' hydrology and its impact on the freshwater of south Florida; used kayaks to collect water samples in the local canals, and learned how to use aquatic sampling and analysis equipment, also designing an experiment to try and detect the presence of optical brighteners and bacteria in the water samples; investigated current environmental issues in the Keys, such as the status of the Key Deer, cruise ships dumping, property and development rights, and conch, sponge and lobster fishing; learned about the natural history of the area including mangrove islands, coral reefs, coastal hammocks and rocky intertidal zones; and examined other major coastal zone issues from the scientific, technological and societal perspectives, such as how human activity including overpopulation, urban sprawl, and marine debris, is impacting these fragile environments. We also investigated the impacts of the citrus and sugar cane industries on the water and air quality of central and southern Florida and staff from the U.S. Army Corps of Engineers filled us in on the current status of the Everglades Restoration Project. Back in Maryland we studied the freshwater systems of the Chesapeake Bay watershed including how natural and human forces can alter the water quality of streams and rivers draining into the Bay. Now we find ourselves at the last leg of the semester at the Chesapeake Biological Laboratory (CBL), part of the University of Maryland System, located in Solomon's Island, at the mouth of the Patuxent River. Here we continue to study the estuarine ecology of the Chesapeake Bay and its tidal rivers. We have also visited SERC several times where I was happy to see how my oyster research project was being continued by the scientists there. **(Again, I surely don't understand it all the way Alexandra does, but I like hearing the details.)**

This year I am also Treasurer of the Environmental Club in my college and am working to set up a national honor society for environmental science students. Through the Club, I help organize and participate in environmental activities such as the Carol Creek Restoration Project, helping to plant new trees and clean up the creek bed or partnering with the Chesapeake Bay Foundation in their Farm Stewardship Program to restore a degraded section of Creagers Branch near its entrance to the Monocacy River.

As a laboratory assistant in their Biology Department, I put new knowledge into practice by helping to prepare solutions and media, setup and takedown lab experiments, carry out general maintenance of teaching, research and prep labs among other duties. During winter break I met with the head of the Tiputini Research Station in Ecuador, who introduced me to the coordinator of the University of San Francisco's campus on the Galapagos Islands where I hope to go study a semester during my junior year to learn about the unique conservation issues affecting the islands. As a member of the Atlantic Estuarine Research Society, I volunteered last year at their Water Monitoring in Estuaries meeting. This past year, among other awards I was the Department of Energy's Environmental Scholar and won scholarships to attend the National Hispanic Environmental Council Annual Meeting, in Seattle, WA and the 2005 NOPHNRCSE Annual Meeting and Training Conference in Lafayette, LA, where I was also awarded an additional scholarship. Through these conference I was approached by many government institutions offering summer jobs and I accepted an offer through the USDA's STEP Program to work as a Wildlife biotechnician with the U.S. Forest Serve at Mt. Hood National Forest in Oregon. There my area of research will focus on the forest owl population.

(Again, as it relates to GMS principles: there's no doubt that Alexandra is passionate about what she's doing with her time and where she's going in life. Clearly we've got the makings of a long and dedicated career with environmental issues, and that's something judges admire.)

Among other activities I have done in the past to prepare me to reach my life goals, I did biomedical research at the University of Maryland's Medical Center the summer after I graduated from high school. The project included weekly tutoring of underprivileged inner city children in Baltimore. During my sophomore year in high school I volunteered at the Smithsonian National Zoo, where I prepared special diets for the animals, cleaned the cages, did research on ants (which won me first prize in Zoology at the science fair), and served as a guide. In earlier years, I participated in activities at the Mountain Institute (mountain ecosystem preservation) and the Marine Science Consortium (Marine Biology coursework).

I also think that the outdoor activities I love will be a big help to me. These include kayaking, rock climbing, outdoor survival, hiking, orienteering, rappelling, obstacle courses, first aid, etc. I hope to work in isolated areas and it is important to be in good physical condition, know how to use a compass, and have basic notions of first aid in order to live in some of these areas.

(Again, normally I would say that personal interests aren't really relevant in a scholarship application, but here, these interests dovetail nicely with her chosen career, so they're definitely worth the mention.)

Being captain of my high school Raider Team and Commander of the Color Guard, further helped me hone my leadership and outdoor survival skills, eventually leading me to be chosen Ms. JROTC by my peers and to win the Daughter's of the American Revolution Medal. During Leadership Training at Fort A.P. Hill I was especially proud to be chosen among 680 cadets to be Company commander! I have also received several awards, scholarships and certificates for the hundreds of hours of community service I was able to carry out during high school. I have learned that giving back is very important and I believe that environmental restoration is one of the great gifts we can give back not only to the community, but to the world.

In the future, I also hope to be a mentor to other Hispanics and minorities wishing to enter into the sciences, lecturing and offering my nonprofit for them to do internships. I wish to share my love of nature with the rest of humanity, educating the public about the importance of our different environments and what we can do to preserve them. I know I envision a big future, but as Eleanor Roosevelt said "The future belongs to those who believe in the beauty of their dreams."

(Overall, very well done. Tons of details, tons of passion and quite a nice blueprint for her career and life plans. As I said in the book, judges like to give money to people whom they feel confident will follow through on their chosen path and succeed, and I see every indication of that in Alexandra's

essay.)

Priscilla Vu

From a young age, I was fascinated by the workings of the world. I would spend hours and hours in the afternoon sun picking grass blades and petals apart while watching the birds, lizards, and snails meander around me in a constantly active world. I knew since then, that science was something that would allow me to look deeper into the world, and something that would become a passion. For that reason, I began looking within my community for opportunities to explore science, and applied to volunteer at Western Medical Center. **(A nice, simple introduction. Nothing earth-shattering, just a nice, clean setting of the scene displaying a refreshing love for science. Which, by the way, the U.S. is sorely lacking among its students in the 21st century!)**

Walking through the empty corridors, I passed doors and doors each day as I began volunteering at Western Medical Center. At first, I did not feel that my tasks at Western Medical Center were as fulfilling as I had hoped. I would spend hours restacking the bookcase in the playroom without ever actually seeing the children. I would restock the towels and soap dispensers without ever actually seeing the patients. I would put together baby cribs without ever actually seeing the baby. I felt distanced from the world as I did these routine tasks on my first few days of volunteering.

However, one day, I came up to the nurse and asked her if she needed any help. She handed me a few jugs and asked me to walk around into the patient rooms and ask if they would like anything more to drink. Excitedly, I entered into the rooms, finally able to step beyond remote corridors and pass through the doors that had seemed like barriers at first. I came in, and was shocked when the patient asked for "jugo." I had no idea what she meant at first, even though I knew it was Spanish. After awhile, however, I learned that "jugo" meant juice. Eventually, I began to communicate with these patients with the minimal Spanish I had learned from school, asking them things like how they were feeling and making small talk. I moved around between the two units I was trained in, the Pediatrics and Mother/Baby Unit, and continued communicating with nurses and patients on a daily basis. My Spanish improved with each discussion I had, and I finally was able to break the distance I had initially felt with the patients. I brought toys to little kids and watched their eyes widen in excitement. Even bringing a new towel or cranberry juice to a new mother would brighten her day. Their thank you's and appreciation were so rewarding that it inspired me to want a future career where I would be able to help and interact with others. That initial experience at Western Medical Center led me to choose medicine as a potential future. **(Overall, a nice lead-in to a more serious discussion of her medical plans. Nothing too heavy here, which is fine, but there's a certain simplicity and sincerity that I can't put my finger on. But it's there.)**

After determining medicine as a potential future, I applied to a prestigious Kaiser Permanente Internship and was accepted. Every Tuesday and Thursday, I would take time after school to attend the classes about electrocardiograms, CPR, intibations, suturing, injections, etc. However, the most valuable aspect of this internship was the shadowing I did each week. Each week, I would be assigned a physician, technician, or nurse to shadow. My favorite people to shadow were the physicians. **(A smart move to point out that she chose to do this after school during the week. This is a good job of the whole "While my friends were out having fun..." issue that I address in the "Confessions" book. As a judge, I'm impressed that she gave up her time to go do this after school, and I didn't need her to point out what the other kids were out doing in order to make her point.)**

Each physician I shadowed had something new to show me. A few physicians allowed me to watch his or her one-to-one interactions with the patients. Each patient that came in had a new story to tell. Many patients could only list symptoms while the doctor was required to be the detective in determining the problem. One patient came in refusing to quit cigarettes, demanding the doctor to permit his senior home to allow him to smoke again. I watched these doctors work on the spot, recalling knowledge from the top of their heads in a way that best suits their patients. I admire how versatile and tolerant the physician had to be, and his or her ability to interact with the many different patients that come in each day. These physicians became people I admired. I also liked how each day would be different because of the different patients and ailments that would come in. This enjoyable experience inspired me to further explore the field of science. **(Did Tiffany mean to say "medicine" here instead of "science"? I'm not sure. "Science" is pretty broad. I'll give her the benefit of the doubt.)**

Another physician I shadowed was Vietnamese like me. She told me stories about how she traveled each year to Vietnam to give free healthcare and immunizations to impoverished people in Vietnam. She has been one of the most inspirational figures in my life. I admired her ability to work such a prestigious job while also volunteering hours back to the community. Many people with the qualifications and ability to greatly help a large amount of people often do not. **(Amen. A mature observation.)** I want to be one of those people in the future who will be generous enough to take time out of my life to give back to the community.

Probably one of the most poignant medical experiences I have ever experienced, however, was standing by the side of my grandpa as he laid in his deathbed. On the car ride to the hospital, I sat in the car repeating to myself, "I will not cry. I will not cry." But the instant I walked into that room and saw my grandpa laying on the bed, susceptible to his lung failure, my eyes began to flood with tears.

Surrounded by family, it was during this moment that I decided that I wanted a future in which I could help prevent at least one person from grieving. My grandfather's mind was completely healthy, but he had no control over the physical ailments of his body. His death inspired me to be stronger, and to grow into a person that could aid those in need. It was from this experience that I learned of the poignant effects a medical ailment could not only have on an individual but on the individual's family also.

Aside from personal reasons, medicine is also something that is academically enticing. I have always loved science, especially lab work. When given the opportunity to grow intellectually in something I'm passionate about, I never let that opportunity pass by. **(I'm glad she mentions this part, because it really sets her apart from a lot of the applicants with aspirations to become doctors. You hear a lot about wanting to help people, help ease suffering, etc. -- all very noble, of course -- but you rarely hear a person come out and say how eager they are to attack the difficult science work that's involved in becoming a doctor.)** When other students would scribble down last minute answers for a lab, I would turn in a typed lab that took hours to complete. Although these other students would get close to full credit, I did not feel frustrated or less motivated to work hard. **(Hey, I just gave you praise for not doing this earlier! Remember, Readers: this would've read just as well had she just mentioned her own above-and-beyond efforts in the lab and not her slacker classmates.)** Although my AP Biology teacher and AP Physics teachers have personally commended my labs, their praise isn't a prime motivation. My prime motivation comes from within myself and my passion for learning. I feel that by spending those extra few hours to challenge myself and be thorough, I am not wasting time, but am allowing myself to grow intellectually in a